Eufemia Azzolina Pupella

SICILIAN COOKERY

Bread and Pizzas, Appetiters, Pasta, Soup and Rice Dishes, Sauces, Meat, Fish, Desserts and Confectionery

TWO HUNDRED AND TWELVE TRIED AND TESTED RECIPES,
WITH ILLUSTRATIONS, ANNOTATIONS,
VARIATIONS AND SUGGESTIONS

PHOTOGRAPHS BY
PIER SILVIO ONGARO

BONECHI

Editorial conception: CASA EDITRICE BONECHI

Project and production: ANTEPRIMA

Translated by: STEPHANIE JOHNSON

American measurements by: LORA VEZZOSI

Photolitho: LA COMPOSIZIONE

ISBN 88-8029-596-9

The photographs in this book were taken specially by Pier Silvio Ongaro, Agenzia Polis, at the Ristorante "A cuccagna" in Palermo.

A TAVOLA SI SCORDANO LI TRIVULI

(Tribulations are forgotten at the dinner table)

E. Alaimo "Proverbi Siciliani" Edit. Martello

*For my children Silvano,
Marco, Massimo,
Mario and Sandra*

Why a book of Sicilian recipes? For just over thirty years I have lived with my family in Milan. Many of our friends are not Sicilian and they have always appreciated the dishes prepared for them and many a time have they spurred me on to collect together the recipes for our dishes.

I accordingly decided to collect and select the recipes, all hand-written on faded pages and kept in boxes - some of them quite precious - inherited by my family and that of my husband, almost as if the secret of a gastronomic heritage was to be preserved.

I did not confine myself just to our families' recipes, but the collaboration of friends and relatives who live in different areas of Sicily was also sought.

The material gathered together is vast owing to the variety in the dishes. There are very rich, elaborate recipes which require hours and hours of work, and there are simple recipes which are at the same time nutritious. In fact, there are two types of home cuisine in Sicily: the baronial or "monzu" (Italianised from the French "monsieur" as the cook used to be called) and the daily fare of the people.

The status symbol for the rich and noble was being overweight; indeed, gout was the disease of the powerful. The peasant, the fisherman and the miner could only afford meat sometimes on Sundays or during the feasting on celebration days, religious or otherwise. The longer-living Sicilians belonged to the latter category. I have collected the recipes of the simple folk for two reasons. Theirs is a healthy cuisine, varied and fragrant, being based on vegetables and without animal fat. Condiments often have uncooked olive oil as their base. The second reason is that many of these recipes are quite simple to make up, though at the same time fanciful.

It is for this reason that dietologists have, for quite a few years now, recommended this type of cuisine as an example of correct, balanced nutriment, referred to (even abroad) as the "Mediterranean diet". I have purposefully introduced two or three recipes of baronial cooking as an example of the cuisine used only on important occasions.

The great variety in Sicilian recipes is due to the difficulties in communication that existed between one area of Sicily and another. In fact, local products

alone found use in the kitchen. Sicily's history has, for many centuries, been characterised by the domination of heterogeneous civilisations which have left their mark not only on the territory but on the culinary traditions of the island. Therefore, in the ingredients and in the dishes enriched with the inventiveness of the Sicilians, it is possible to find traces of the different peoples who have followed each other on Sicilian soil. Over time, every domination imported their own seeds and spices.

While carrying out this research, I was fascinated to peruse Sicily's course of history and customs through her gastronomy. The presence of the Greek civilisation can be seen in the usage of green and black olives, salted ricotta cheese, the Homeric lamb grilled over charcoal, fish, honey and, above all, wine, the production of which was begun by the first Greek colonisers. Going back to the Roman period, when Sicily was considered the granary of Italy, are the "maccu di fave" (mashed broad beans, from the Latin "maccare"), stuffed cuttlefish, baked onions seasoned with oil and vinegar, sausages and the "sanguinacci" or blood sausages which were always very much appreciated at the sumptuous banquets given at the Villa del Casale in Piazza Armerina.

After the fall of the Roman Empire, Sicily was not spared invasion by Northern peoples (the Franks and the Goths) who, however, did not stay long enough to leave a mark on the culinary art. On the other hand, the Byzantines imported a few spices from the East which continue to be consumed today. From the architectural and cultural points of view, the island recovered all

its splendour with the Arabs and flourished once more. Great innovations were also made with regard to the cuisine and dishes became increasingly varied and sophisticated. Thanks to the introduction of the cultivation of sugar cane, refined sugar became the principle ingredient of a good many sweet dishes (such as the "royal paste" or marzipan) and,

associated with ricotta and the candied peel of oranges and lemons (it was indeed the Arabs who imported the cultivation of citrus fruit), allowed the famous cassata to be concocted. The use of mulberries, aniseed, sesame and some spices such as cinnamon and saffron goes back precisely to this period. Sorbets were prepared with essences from fruit and flowers and the snow carried down from Mount Etna, and the ice-cream that can still today be found in the Trapani area was made with jasmine oil. The most obvious trace of the encounter with the Arabian civilisation is couscous in the zone around Trapani, differing from the North African dish only in that it is served with a fish soup.

The period of the Norman conquest is responsible for the use of salted cod and salted and smoked herrings. After the incident of the Sicilian Vespers in 1282 and the consequent liberation by the Angevins who had succeeded to the Normans, the Kingdom of Sicily was constituted and it was in this period that the distinction began between the nobles' or baronial cuisine (so-called "monzu"), which had castles and convents as a setting, and popular cooking which developed in taverns and inns. The distinction between these cuisines is often not so obvious because the name of the dish is the same, but the ingredients and how it is served differ.

Following the arrival of the Spaniards, these two types of cuisine continued along parallel tracks, both of them introducing the use of the tomato from America which goes so well with aubergines, onions and sweet peppers, whereas the wild fennel used in so many recipes originally came from the Canary Islands.

Today, with the facility of commercial exchange and preservation by deep freezing, gastronomic customs have also changed.

We are no longer scandalised if a restaurant in Catania or Palermo includes tagliatelle with a ham-and-cream sauce on the menu. Only the tagliatelle in this dish are truly Sicilian, provided they are fresh and home-made.

Just as ham and cream are used in Sicily, so markets in the North of Italy have the ingredients of Sicilian cuisine, such as wild fennel leaves, capers, oregano and "caciocavallo" cheese. Talking about "caciocavallo", I have found it - just think - in the United States, at Santa Clara in California. My husband and I were staying with friends and, on the occasion of a party in our honour, I thought of preparing "arancini" (rice patties). My American friends escorted me to a supermarket of Italian food. I found "caciocavallo" which often cannot be found in the North of Italy! To this regard, I have indicated a few alternatives for ingredients which are not always easily available in markets and shops.

Thanks

I wish to thank Simona Abriani, who had faith in this book, and the Iten sisters, particularly Marlene, who tracked down the photographer. He is from Verona, but he lives in Sicily and has absorbed a huge amount of "Sicilianness", knowing how to understand and appreciate all the nuances and contradictions of this complex land, which precisely for this reason is so fascinating. I am grateful to Bianca Maria Fumagalli for her very valid critical help and for having transcribed the whole work. I also give thanks to Peppa Anaclerio for her search for old recipes.

Finally, I wish to thank all those friends who were "guinea pigs" for the dishes that I had never prepared before and all those who gave me useful advice.

Restaurant proprietors: Francesco Paolo and Carmelo Sammarco

The pastry cook: Anna Sammarco

Index

PASTA, SOUP AND RICE DISHES

SAUCES

MEAT

FISH

FISH (CONTINUOUS)

DESSERTS AND CONFECTIONERY

Notes and Suggestion to Readers:

- **QUANTITIES IN THE RECIPES ARE CALCULATED FOR FOUR TO SIX SERVINGS.**

- METRIC MEASUREMENTS ARE GIVEN FIRST, FOLLOWED BY IMPERIAL AND FINALLY THOSE FOR AMERICAN READERS. I STRONGLY RECOMMEND STICKING TO THE SAME GROUP OF MEASUREMENTS THROUGHOUT THE RECIPE.

- FOR DISHES WHICH REQUIRE BAKING OR ROASTING, I HAVE INCLUDED THE TERMS "MODERATE OVEN" = 150°-160°C / 300°-325°F/GAS MARK 2-3 AND "HOT OVEN" 180°C-200°C/350°-400°F/GAS MARK 4-6.

- MENTION IS MADE OF VARIOUS ITALIAN CHEESES. IF YOU CANNOT FIND THE "GENUINE ARTICLE", HERE IS A BASIC DESCRIPTION TO HELP YOU DECIDE ON WORTHY SUBSTITUTES:
  PARMESAN CHEESE IS THE HARD, DRY CHEESE KNOWN WORLD-WIDE AS A COMPLEMENT TO MANY DISHES AND NEEDING NO INTRODUCTION HERE;
  PECORINO IS A HARD OR SEMI-HARD SHEEP'S MILK CHEESE AND IS AVAILABLE AT VARYING STAGES OF RIPENING;
  MADE FROM EWE'S MILK, **RICOTTA** IS SOFT AND FRESH, LOOKING RATHER LIKE COTTAGE CHEESE;
  PRIMOSALE IS A FRESH, COMPACT CHEESE;
  PROVOLA IS A SEMI-HARD CHEESE MADE FROM BUFFALO MILK, EATEN FRESH OR SMOKED;
  PROVOLONE IS A MILD OR SHARP HARD CHEESE WHICH IS USUALLY SMOKED;
  CACIOCAVALLO IS THE SAME KIND OF CHEESE AS PROVOLONE;
  THE **CACIOTTA** MENTIONED IN THIS BOOK IS MADE FROM EWE'S MILK IN TUSCANY AND SARDINIA AND COULD AT A PINCH BE SUBSTITUTED WITH GRUYÈRE.

- QUANTITIES FOR HERBS ARE NOT DEFINED. IT DEPENDS ON PERSONAL TASTE AND THE INTENSITY OF THEIR AROMA. BASIL LOSES ITS FRAGRANCE WHEN DRIED, SO DOSES WILL BE LARGER THAN WITH FRESH BASIL. OREGANO IS FREQUENTLY USED IN MEDITERRANEAN COOKING. IT MAY BE SUBSTITUTED WITH LESS PUNGENT MARJORAM. WILD FENNEL MAY BE REPLACED BY THE LEAFY TOPS OF BULB FENNEL.

- UNLESS SPECIFIED, USE INDIFFERENTLY ANCHOVIES PRESERVED IN OIL OR SALT.

- WHERE MENTION IS MADE OF OIL, I REFER TO EXTRA VERGINE OLIVE OIL, WHICH IS ESSENTIAL IN SICILIAN COOKING FOR FLAVOURING DISHES. THOUGH IDEAL FOR FRYING AS WELL, OTHER VEGETABLE OILS MAY BE USED IN DIFFERENT CLIMES.

- A VANILLA FLAVOURING CAN BE ACHIEVED EITHER WITH A SACHET OF VANILLA POWDER (ABOUT 0.5G / ¼ TSP), A HALF TO ONE TEASPOON OF VANILLA EXTRACT, OR IN THE TRADITIONAL WAY BY STEEPING A POD (BEAN) IN LIQUID; KEPT IN A DRY JAR, IT CAN BE USED AGAIN.

- 30G (1OZ) OF FRESH BREWER'S YEAST CAN BE SUBSTITUTED WITH ONE-AND-A-HALF PACKETS OF ACTIVE DRIED YEAST.

- TOMATOES ARE EASY TO PEEL IF YOU PUT THEM IN A HOT OVEN FOR FIVE MINUTES. ALLOW THE SKINS TO COOL. THEY WILL WRINKLE UP AND COME AWAY EASILY FROM THE PULP.

British/American Glossary

AUBERGINE / EGGPLANT	GREASEPROOF PAPER / WAX PAPER
BAIN-MARIE / WATER BATH	GRILL / BROIL
BAKING TIN / BAKING PAN	HOTPLATE / GRIDDLE
BICARBONATE OF SODA / BAKING SODA	ICING SUGAR / CONFECTIONER'S SUGAR
BROAD BEANS / FAVA BEANS	MINCED MEAT / GROUND MEAT
CHICK PEAS / GARBANZOS	PULSES / LEGUMES
COURGETTES / ZUCCHINI	SPRING ONION / SCALLION
CORNFLOUR / CORNSTARCH	TINNED / CANNED
GLACÉ ICING / FROSTING	VANILLA POD / VANILLA BEAN

BREAD AND PIZZAS

*T*here is a wide variety of bread in Sicily, both in the making and in the fanciful shape of the loaves. Bread is never lacking even in the poorest homes. It must always be in plentiful supply and if it becomes stale ("*pani duru mantiene la casa*" - bread solves all household problems), it is used in soups, croquettes and stuffings. Fried breadcrumbs, for example, with salty sardines and wild fennel, become a tasty sauce for spaghetti. (With the characteristic Sicilian sense of humour, the poor man's version of this dish has been baptised "*pasta with the sardines still in the sea*" - in fact, among all the ingredients of the famous sardine pasta dish, it is precisely the sardines which are lacking!).

Idioms concerning bread are numerous. In its dramatic force, one of them expresses the most dire poverty:

"*Si avissi pignateddu, ogghiu e sali,*
facissi pani cuttu; Si avissi pani!"
(If I had a small saucepan, oil and salt,
I would cook some bread soup… If I had some bread!)

Other locutions which convey the sacredness of bread are: "*Pani e fami*" and "*Pani e cuteddu*", i.e. Bread [to serve] with hunger, Bread and a knife [to cut it with]. These expressions convey the absolute lack of accompaniments for bread. Before covering it up and leaving to prove, housewives would inscribe a cross on the top of the loaf and kiss it, thus fulfilling a propitious rite which ended with the insertion of the loaf into the hot oven, accompanying the gesture with litanies proposed by the eldest, with all the others joining in to sing the chorus:

"*Sant'Agostino ogni pane quantu un cufino*
Santa Rita beddu di crusta e beddu di muddica
Sant'Isidoro beddu dintra e beddu fora"
(St. Augustine make every loaf as large as a cufino*
St. Rita make the bread fine of crust and fine of crumb
St. Isidore make the bread fine within and fine without)

Baking day, which usually fell on Friday, was a joyous day ("*Beniditta ch'idda pasta/ca di venniti s'impasta*" - Blessed is the dough prepared on Friday). So as to exploit the hot oven to the utmost, various types of pizza and stuffed "calzone" (a Neapolitan savoury roll) were prepared and the bread was eaten just out of the oven, seasoned with oil and/or olives, cheese and what the larder offered, allowing the combinations to spring from the imagination.

(*) *The basket of woven palm leaves which was used in the kitchen as a container. By extension, it was considered a symbol of plenteousness.*

CALZONE ALLA PALERMITANA
SAVOURY ROLL PALERMO-STYLE

◆

- 1 KG / 2 LBS /LEAVENED BREAD DOUGH
- 200 G / 8 OZ MINCED (GROUND) BEEF
- 200 G / 8 OZ MINCED (GROUND) PORK
- 1 MEDIUM-SIZED ONION
- 30 G / 1 OZ PLAIN (SEMI-SWEET) CHOCOLATE, GRATED
- 30 G / 1 OZ / ¼ CUP CHOPPED, TOASTED ALMONDS
- 3 EGG WHITES AND 1 YOLK
- 125 ML / 4 FL OZ / ½ CUP WHITE WINE

◆

PREPARATION TIME: 1 HOUR

CHOP THE ONION and fry gently in oil. Add the pork and beef, season with salt and pepper and mix well. Pour on the wine and allow to evaporate. Add the grated chocolate and the almonds.

Cook over a low heat for 30 minutes, stirring from time to time in order to prevent the mixture from sticking to the bottom of the pan.

Before drawing off the heat, slowly fold in the stiffly-beaten egg whites.

Divide the dough into two parts. Roll out with a rolling pin to form two discs. Oil a baking tin or a round baking pan and line with one of the discs.

Pour over the meat sauce and cover with the other disc, pressing the edges together well. Prick the surface with a fork to allow the steam to escape. Brush the pie with the beaten egg yolk and bake in a hot oven for about 20 minutes.

CALZONE DI MODICA
SAVOURY ROLL MODICA-STYLE

◆

- 1 KG / 2 LBS LEAVENED BREAD DOUGH
- 300 G / ¾ LB FRESH PECORINO CHEESE
- 6 ANCHOVY FILLETS
- 1 TBSP LARD OR 125 ML / 4 FL OZ / ½ CUP OLIVE OIL

◆

PREPARATION TIME: 1 HOUR

KNEAD THE LEAVENED dough with the lard or oil and divide into two parts. Oil a baking tin or dish and line with one of the dough sections. Arrange a layer of cheese slices and pieces of anchovy, sprinkle with a little pepper and cover with the remaining dough. With your fingers dampened in water, press the edges together well. Prick the top of the pie with a fork and bake for about 30 minutes in a hot oven until it has turned golden.

VARIATION: the stuffing may be made with slices of tomato and fresh pecorino cheese, or ricotta and skinned, cooked sausage, or parsley and anchovies, or else ricotta and boiled spinach mixed together with a seasoning of salt and pepper, or even onion lightly sautéed in oil. Use your imagination to raid the larder.

CALZONE DI RAGUSA
SAVOURY ROLL RAGUSA-STYLE

- 1 KG / 2 LBS LEAVENED BREAD DOUGH
- 1 KG / 2 LBS BONED LAMB
- 3 SMALL ONIONS
- 1 TBSP TOMATO CONCENTRATE
- 125 ML / 4 FL OZ / ½ CUP RED WINE
- 1 EGG YOLK
- SALT
- PEPPER
- OLIVE OIL

PREPARATION TIME: 1 HOUR

FIRST BROWN THE CHOPPED onion in oil in a pan, then add the pieces of lamb. Pour on the wine and let it evaporate. Add the tomato concentrate dissolved in hot water, season with salt and pepper and leave to cook for about 20 minutes. Oil a baking tin or dish and line with half of the leavened dough. Pour the stew over and cover with the other half of the dough, pressing the edges together with your water-moistened fingers. Prick the pie over with a fork and brush with the beaten egg yolk. Bake in a hot oven for 20-30 minutes.

VARIATION: this dish is prepared on Christmas Eve in Caltanisetta, but there the dough is stuffed with fillets of fried salt cod in a tomato and onion sauce. In Messina, on the other hand, the dish is still made on Christmas Eve, but the filling is made of fried pork sausage, slices of fresh pecorino cheese, spring onions and black olives.

CRESPELLE DI RICOTTA E ACCIUGHE
RICOTTA AND ANCHOVY FRITTERS

◆

- 1 KG / 2 LBS / 6½ CUPS FLOUR
- 50 G / 2 OZ / FRESH BREWER'S YEAST
- 500 G / 1 LB RICOTTA CHEESE
- 6-7 ANCHOVY FILLETS
- LARD OR OIL FOR FRYING

◆

PREPARATION TIME: 2½ HOURS

IN A BOWL, mix the flour together with the brewer's yeast dissolved in warm water and season with salt and pepper. Knead the dough, adding more warm water if necessary. When you have obtained a springy paste, cover with a napkin and a woollen cloth and leave for about 2 hours to rise. In the meantime, cut the anchovies up small and put them in a bowl. In another bowl, crush the ricotta with a fork. When the dough has risen, break off a little and, on the palm of your left hand (previously dampened with water), form a shell. In the hollow, put a piece of anchovy and a tablespoon of ricotta. Pull the same dough up to cover the filling and form a ball or an oval. Pour the oil or lard into a deep-sided frying pan and, when hot, arrange the "crespelle" in it with the aid of a spatula. Fry until golden, dry the "crespelle" on kitchen paper and serve hot.

PANE CALDO CONDITO
HOT SEASONED BREAD

- 1 LOAF OF BREAD STRAIGHT OUT OF THE OVEN
- EXTRA-VIRGIN OLIVE OIL
- SALT
- FRESHLY-GROUND PEPPER

PREPARATION TIME: 30 MINUTES

CONNOISSEURS TELL us that bread must not be cut with a knife when still hot from the oven because it would acquire a metallic flavour. It should, instead, be opened up in your fingers or with a length of clean string. Make slits in the crumb of the two halves and season with oil, salt and pepper. Cover with the other half, pressing your fingers down on the crust in order to spread the oil over both surfaces.

VARIATION: the following may be added to the oil, salt and pepper: a pinch of oregano and/or slices of fresh tomato, anchovies, slices of fresh pecorino or fresh caciocavallo cheese, or else pitted green or black olives. The seasoning is left to your imagination and what you have on your shelves. Another variant can be made with left-over bread which is no longer very fresh; slice the bread and soak in a glass of milk. Fry in hot oil and garnish with a slice of primosale cheese and a little piece of anchovy.

PANE CON I FICHI
FIG BREAD

- 500 G / 1 LB / 3 CUPS HARD-GRAINED FLOUR (OR 800 G / 1¾ LBS LEAVENED BREAD DOUGH)
- 25 G / 1 OZ /FRESH BREWER'S YEAST
- 2 TBSP LARD OR OLIVE OIL
- 300 G / ¾ LB DRIED FIGS

PREPARATION TIME: 3 HOURS

WORK THE BREWER'S yeast, two tablespoons of oil, a pinch of salt and some warm water into the flour until you get a smooth dough. Sprinkle with flour, cover with a napkin and a woollen cloth and allow to prove for 2 hours. Cut the figs into pieces and incorporate into the risen dough. Shape as you wish into loaves, place on an oiled baking tray and bake for 30-40 minutes in a hot oven.

VARIATION: instead of figs, you may use raisins or olives or nuts.

PIZZA FRITTA
FRIED PIZZA

◆

- 1 KG / 2 LBS LEAVENED BREAD DOUGH
- 300 G / ¾ LB PRIMOSALE OR OTHER FRESH CHEESE
- 2-3 SMALL TENDER ONIONS
- 4 ANCHOVY FILLETS
- SALT
- LARD OR OLIVE OIL

◆

PREPARATION TIME: 30 MINUTES

SFINCIONE DI CALTANISETTA
SICILIAN PIZZA FROM CALTANISETTA

◆

- 1 KG / 2 LBS LEAVENED BREAD DOUGH
- 1 KG / 2 LBS FRESH TOMATOES
- 1 KG / 2 LBS ONIONS
- 150 G / 6 OZ / 1 CUP BLACK OLIVES
- 1 BUNCH OF BASIL
- 5 ANCHOVIES
- 3 CLOVES OF GARLIC
- 150 G / 6 OZ PRIMOSALE CHEESE
- 50 G / 2 OZ / ½ CUP GRATED PECORINO OR PARMESAN CHEESE

◆

PREPARATION TIME: 1 HOUR

WORK THE LARD or olive oil into the leavened dough, divide into six parts and leave to rise again for a couple of hours. Press out the pieces of dough to form little discs which you will fill with a little chopped onion, cheese slices and pieces of anchovy. Fold each disc over onto itself and press the edges well together with your fingers dampened in water. Fry in hot oil.

VARIATION: at Trapani, another type of pizza is made with leavened dough.
Spread the dough over the bottom of an oiled baking tray or dish and brush the surface with oil. Season with salt, pepper, 3 chopped cloves of garlic, oregano and rosemary. Bake for 20 minutes in a hot oven.

SWEAT THE FINELY-SLICED onion in the oil without letting it fry. Skin the tomatoes, remove the seeds and cut into pieces. Season with salt, pepper and chopped basil. Leave to cook for 15-20 minutes. Line an oiled baking dish with the risen dough and trickle over some oil which you will spread with your hand. Make little hollows here and there with your fingers and insert pieces of garlic, black olives and anchovies. Cover with a layer of primosale cut into pieces and smother with the cooked tomato sauce. Sprinkle the grated cheese over and season with a trickle of oil. Bake for 30 minutes in a hot oven.

SFINCIONE DI PALERMO
SICILIAN PIZZA FROM PALERMO

- 500 G / 1 LB LEAVENED BREAD DOUGH
- 500 G / 1 LB FRESH TOMATOES OR 1 TIN (CAN) OF SKINNED TOMATOES
- 100 G / 4 OZ FRESH CACIOCAVALLO OR PROVOLA OR OTHER SAVOURY CHEESE
- 50 G / 2 OZ / ½ CUP GRATED PECORINO OR PARMESAN CHEESE
- 50 G / 2 OZ / ½ CUP DRY BREADCRUMBS
- 4 ANCHOVY FILLETS
- 1 MEDIUM-SIZED ONION
- BUNCH OF CHOPPED PARSLEY
- 125 ML / 4 FL OZ / ½ CUP OF OLIVE OIL
- SALT
- PEPPER

PREPARATION TIME: 2 HOURS

WORK A GLASS of olive oil and the grated cheese into the leavened dough. Leave to prove for about an hour, wrapped in a woollen cloth.

Meanwhile, in a little oil in a frying pan, gently fry the sliced onion, then add the parsley and the skinned tomatoes, cut into pieces. Season with salt and pepper and leave to simmer over low heat for 20 minutes. At this point, add the anchovies cut into pieces and the sliced caciocavallo or other cheese. Mix well and draw off the heat. In an oiled, deep-sided baking tin or dish, spread out the paste to the thickness of about an inch-and-a-quarter. With your fingers, make a few holes in the top, pour over half the sauce and bake in a hot oven. After about 15 minutes, take the tin out, pour in the remaining sauce and dredge with fried breadcrumbs. Trickle over a little oil and replace in the oven for 30 minutes.

SFINCIONE DI PATATE
SICILIAN POTATO PIZZA

- 500 G / 1 LB POTATOES
- 500 G / 1 LB / 3½ CUPS FLOUR
- 100 G / 4 OZ / FRESH BREWER'S YEAST
- 200 G / 8 OZ SALAMI
- 200 G / 8 OZ PRIMOSALE CHEESE
- 50 G / 2 OZ / ½ CUP DRY BREADCRUMBS

PREPARATION TIME: 2½ HOURS

BOIL THE POTATOES IN SALTED WATER, peel and put through a potato ricer. Heap the purée on a pastry board with the flour and add the yeast dissolved in warm water.
Knead well, adding warm water, if necessary, to obtain a smooth mixture. Dust with flour, wrap the dough up in a napkin, cover with a woollen cloth and leave to prove for two hours.
Oil a baking tin or dish and line the bottom with half the dough, pressing it down with your fingers. On top, arrange one layer of sliced salami and one with most of the primosale cheese slices. Cover with the other half of the dough and a few more slices of cheese. Sprinkle some dry breadcrumbs over the top and bake in a hot oven for 20 minutes.

APPETISERS

"Cosa licca sa di picca"
(Little things give little satisfaction)

E. Alaimo *"Proverbi siciliani"* Edit. Martello

Good things must be eaten sparingly
so as not to spoil the appetite.

A starter course did not exist in the old Sicilian cuisine. Many hours before a celebration dinner (whether in the baronial home or that of the common people), the men used to gather together to talk business, sipping wine and nibbling titbits.

Such dishes were based on raw and cooked vegetables: seasoned olives, aubergines (eggplants), courgettes (zucchini) and tomatoes in oil, pickles, salads, timbales and baby omelettes. On the barons' tables, this fare appeared as side dishes to go with the meat and fish or between one course and the next. Whereas in popular kitchens (except on religious feasts and secular holidays), these same dishes were prepared for the main course, after the soups and pasta dishes which were considered of scarce nutritious value.

Included therefore in this chapter are recipes for salads, vegetables, eggs and omelettes.

Omelettes make a very simple dish, quick to get ready, which can solve the problem the hostess faces when she has very little time to come up with a delicious impromptu dinner. The variety is vast and depends on the ingredients lying on the shelves at home and the whim of the cook. Among the wealth of possible recipes, I have chosen two which I find rather unusual and are little known: one with ricotta and one with dry bread crumbs.

CACIOCAVALLO FRITTO CON L'ORIGANO E L'ACETO

FRIED CACIOCAVALLO WITH AN OREGANO AND VINEGAR DRESSING

◆

- 500 G / 1 LB FRESH CACIOCAVALLO CHEESE
- 125 ML / 4 FL OZ / 8 TBSP VINEGAR
- 2 CLOVES OF GARLIC
- OREGANO
- OLIVE OIL

◆

PREPARATION TIME: 30 MINUTES

HEAT A LITTLE OIL IN A FRYING pan with the whole cloves of garlic, which you will remove as soon as they colour. Fry the sliced caciocavallo on both sides, season with salt and pepper and flavour with oregano. Sprinkle the vinegar over and, after a few minutes, turn off the heat.

This dish is eaten at the end of the summer, when shepherds begin to process the cheeses to be ripened.

Fresh caciocavallo can, in fact, only be found at the end of August and the beginning of September.

CAPONATA
AUBERGINE OR EGGPLANT RAGOUT

♦

- **4** AUBERGINES OR EGGPLANTS
- **200** G / **8** OZ / **1 ⅓** CUPS OLIVES
- **50** G / **2** OZ / **¼** CUP CAPERS
- **2** LARGE STICKS OF CELERY
- **1** SOUP LADLE / **4** TBSP HOME-MADE TOMATO SAUCE
- **2** LARGE ONIONS, FINELY-SLICED
- **125** ML / **4** FL OZ / **8** TBSP VINEGAR
- **1** TBSP GRANULATED SUGAR
- A FEW BASIL LEAVES
- OLIVE OIL

♦

PREPARATION TIME: 3 HOURS

DICE THE AUBERGINES and put in a bowl with salted water for about 2 hours. Clean the celery and blanch in salted water for 5 minutes.

Place the capers in a bowl with hot water to draw the salt out and drain after a few minutes. Put the onion in a little oil in a large frying pan, together with the capers and roughly-chopped olives.

Add the sauce, if already made, or else skin four ripe tomatoes, discard the seeds and chop roughly. Stir with a wooden spoon and turn off the heat once a thick sauce has formed. Squeeze the aubergines, dry them carefully and fry in another frying pan.

Fry the celery, cut into small chunks, in the same oil. Put the fried aubergines and celery in the saucepan with the sauce, mix well and blend the flavours for 5 minutes over a low heat. Sprinkle with sugar, pour over the vinegar and, after a few minutes, turn off the heat and cover with the lid. "Caponata" is better served cold in an earthenware bowl and garnished with basil leaves.

CARCIOFI BELLAVISTA IN TEGAME
STUFFED ARTICHOKES

- 6 GLOBE ARTICHOKES
- 100 G / 4 OZ / 1 CUP DRY BREADCRUMBS
- 50 G / 2 OZ / ½ CUP GRATED PECORINO CHEESE
- 2 ANCHOVY FILLETS
- 2 CLOVES OF GARLIC
- 150 G / 6 OZ CACIOCAVALLO OR SHARP PROVOLONE CHEESE
- SPRIG OF PARSLEY
- SALT AND PEPPER
- OLIVE OIL

PREPARATION TIME: 45 MINUTES

PUT THE ANCHOVY FILLETS in a very little oil in a pan and crush them with a fork.

Add the dry breadcrumbs and stir until brown and toasted, turn off the heat and allow to cool to lukewarm before adding the grated cheese and the diced caciocavallo.

Trim the spikes of the artichokes, eliminate the tougher leaves and open them out like a flower. Stuff the artichokes with the prepared breadcrumb mixture.

Place them in a saucepan where you will have lightly coloured the two finely-chopped cloves of garlic.

Pour two glasses of water over the artichokes to cover, leave to simmer gently and, when the water has almost completely evaporated, add the chopped parsley.

CARCIOFI CON IL LIMONE
LEMON-FLAVOURED ARTICHOKE

- 6 GLOBE ARTICHOKES
- 2 CLOVES OF GARLIC
- SPRIG OF PARSLEY
- 1 LEMON
- SALT
- PEPPER
- OLIVE OIL

PREPARATION TIME: 1 HOUR

AFTER TRIMMING THE ARTICHOKES of the tough and spiky parts, slice them and place in a pan with the chopped garlic and parsley, the oil, salt and pepper.

Cover with water and simmer gently. When the vegetable is cooked, pour over the lemon juice and a little fresh parsley.

VARIATION: when the artichokes are ready, pour over 4 eggs, beaten with a fork, instead of the lemon juice. Season with salt, pepper and parsley. This dish may be served as a side plate with boiled or roast meats or game. It used to be a spring-time dish. Deep freezing today concedes us the satisfaction of cooking artichokes in any season of the year, apart from the convenience.

CARCIOFI FRITTI IN PASTELLA
BATTER-FRIED ARTICHOKES

◆

- 4 GLOBE ARTICHOKES
- 2 CLOVES OF GARLIC
- 2 EGGS
- 250 G / 8 OZ / 1⅔ CUPS WHITE FLOUR
- 1 LEMON
- 1 SPRIG PARSLEY
- ¼ TSP FRESH BREWER'S YEAST
- OIL FOR FRYING
- OLIVE OIL

◆

PREPARATION TIME: 1½ HOURS

MAKE THE BATTER BY PUTTING the flour in a bowl and blending it into a little warm water (¼ cup). Add the brewer's yeast, allowing to dissolve, then the egg, beaten with a fork, and season with parsley, chopped garlic, salt and pepper. Leave to rest for 30 minutes. Meanwhile, discard the tough and spiky parts of the artichokes and cut into wedges. Blanch in water with the squeezed lemon juice and a pinch of salt for five minutes. Drain, dry, dip them in the batter and fry them in hot oil.

CARCIOFI IN SFORMATO
TIMBALE OF ARTICHOKE

◆

- 6 GLOBE ARTICHOKES
- ¼ ONION
- 1 SPRIG OF PARSLEY
- 1 CUP OF MEAT STOCK (OR FROM A BOUILLON CUBE)
- 1 EGG
- 50 G / 2 OZ / ½ CUP GRATED CHEESE

◆

PREPARATION TIME: 1 HOUR

TRIM THE ARTICHOKES, removing the tough outer leaves, cut into quarters and boil for 5-10 minutes. Drain and chop up or cut into pieces. Chop the onion and sauté in a little oil, together with the chopped parsley, until coloured.

Put the cooked onion into a bowl with the puréed artichoke. Add the egg, grated cheese, cup of stock, salt and pepper. Blend well and place the mixture in a greased oven tin or dish. Bake in a hot oven for 15 minutes.

VARIATION: you may use the same mixture as a filling in leavened bread dough or in a pie of flaky pastry.

CARDI LESSATI IN PASTELLA
BOILED CARDOONS IN BATTER

- 4 CARDOONS
- 150 G / 6 OZ / 1 CUP FLOUR
- 2 ANCHOVY FILLETS
- 1 EGG
- 15 G / ½ OZ / 1 TBSP FRESH BREWER'S YEAST
- SALT
- OIL FOR FRYING

PREPARATION TIME: 1 HOUR

B OIL THE CARDOONS in salted water and cut into small chunks. Knead the flour in a bowl with a glass of warm water where the yeast has been dissolved. Add the egg (beaten with a fork) and the anchovies in tiny pieces. Leave it all to rest for thirty minutes. Plunge the cardoons into the batter thus obtained, coating them completely, and fry in very hot oil.

VARIATION: serve the boiled cardoons in a vinaigrette dressing. This is a dish to accompany dry broad beans which have been boiled in their skins with a bulb of whole garlic.

"Si vuliti viviri gustusu, ovu di tunnu e carduni spinusu".
(If you want to appreciate wine, sip it with tuna fish roes and cardoons.)
E. Alaimo "Proverbi siciliani"
Edit. Martello.

CAVOLFIORE FRITTO IN PASTELLA
CAULIFLOWER FRIED IN BATTER

◆

- 1 KG / 2 LBS CAULIFLOWER
- 150 G / 6 OZ / 1 CUP FLOUR
- 2 EGGS
- 1 ANCHOVY
- SALT
- PEPPER
- OIL FOR FRYING

◆

PREPARATION TIME: 1 HOUR

BOIL THE CAULIFLOWER IN SALTED WATER. Drain while still crisp and divide into florets. Make the batter by beating the eggs in a bowl with a fork and sprinkling in the flour, being careful that lumps do not form. Continue to stir briskly, always in the same direction. Add the anchovy, cut into tiny pieces, salt and pepper. Dip the cauliflower into the batter and fry in the hot oil in a frying pan.

CAVOLFIORE IN SFORMATO
TIMBALE OF CAULIFLOWER

- 1 KG / 2 LBS CAULIFLOWER
- 2 BOILED POTATOES
- 2 EGGS
- 50 G / 2 OZ / ½ CUP GRATED CHEESE
- 30 G / 1 OZ / 5 TBSP DRY BREADCRUMBS
- 50 G / 2 OZ SALAMI
- 100 G / 4 OZ CACIOCAVALLO OR SHARP PROVOLA CHEESE

PREPARATION TIME: 1½ HOURS

CLEAN THE CAULIFLOWER, cut into quarters and boil in salted water. Put the boiled potatoes and cauliflower through a vegetable mill. Add the eggs, grated cheese, salami and diced caciocavallo or provola cheese to the purée. Amalgamate well and place the mixture in an oiled and crumbed oven dish.
Bake in a hot oven for about 20 minutes.

VARIATION: place half the purée in a greased ovenproof dish. Layer the bottom with fresh, savoury cheese slices and 200 g (8 oz) skinned and crumbled sausage. Cover with the other half of the purée. Sprinkle the dry breadcrumbs over and bake for 20 minutes in a hot oven.

FAVE LESSATE
BOILED BROAD BEANS

PUT THE BEANS to soak overnight after removing the "black eyes" with the aid of a knife. Boil in salted water with the bulb of garlic. When cooked, transfer to a bowl and season with oil and pepper.

- 500 G / 1 LB DRY BROAD BEANS IN THEIR SKINS
- 1 WHOLE BULB OF GARLIC
- SALT
- PEPPER
- OLIVE OIL

PREPARATION TIME: 3 HOURS

VARIATIONS: cook the broad beans with 300 g (¾ lb) of wild fennel, the same weight of Swiss chard and 500 g (1 lb) cardoons. This makes an excellent winter dish. You can also cook the broad beans with just the cardoons. This dish was greatly used in inns and married well with red wine. To this regard, there is a proverb which says "Voi sdivacari tutte le cannete? / Carduni amari e favuzza caliata." (Do you wish to empty all the wine carafes? / Eat baked broad beans and bitter cardoons).

E. Alaimo "Proverbi siciliani" Edit. Martello.

FRITTATA CON IL PANGRATTATO
OMELETTE WITH BREADCRUMBS

◆

- 6 EGGS
- 80 G / 3 OZ / ¾ CUP DRY BREADCRUMBS
- 50 G / 2 OZ / ½ CUP GRATED CHEESE
- CHOPPED PARSLEY
- CHOPPED BASIL
- SALT AND PEPPER
- OLIVE OIL

◆

PREPARATION TIME: 15 MINUTES

BEAT THE EGGS IN A BOWL, add the dry breadcrumbs, the grated cheese and the chopped basil and parsley. Season with salt and pepper. Stir well and pour the mixture into some hot oil in a frying pan.

Cook the omelette on both sides and serve at table. This is a poor man's dish, but tasty and nourishing. Served with courgettes (zucchini) or aubergine (eggplant) prepared under oil, it was the main dish following the soup or pasta course.

VARIATION: try baking the omelette in a moderate oven for a good quarter-of-an-hour.

FRITTATA CON LA RICOTTA

RICOTTA CHEESE OMELETTE

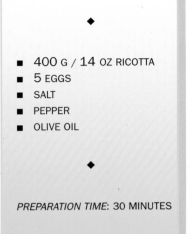

◆

- 400 G / 14 OZ RICOTTA
- 5 EGGS
- SALT
- PEPPER
- OLIVE OIL

◆

PREPARATION TIME: 30 MINUTES

POUR A LITTLE OIL INTO A FRYING PAN and place in it the ricotta, cut into slices. Brown the cheese on both sides. Beat the eggs with a fork, add salt and pepper and pour onto the ricotta. When the omelette has set on one side, turn it over with the help of the saucepan lid and cook on the other side.

VARIATIONS: follow the same procedure with the addition of grated pecorino cheese and a few leaves of chopped parsley. It was also the usage to beat finely-sliced raw vegetables and aromatic herbs (chopped, tender wild fennel, shallots, asparagus, basil, garlic) together with the eggs, but without the cheese. On the other hand, when other vegetables were used (courgettes or zucchini, potatoes, peas, globe artichokes and cauliflower), they were first boiled and then poured into the beaten egg and cooked in the pan.

FRITTATA DOLCE CON LA MARMELLATA
JAM OR MARMALADE OMELETTE

- ◆
- ■ 6 EGGS
- ■ 3 TBSP ORANGE MARMALADE OR APRICOT JAM (OR OF OTHER FRUIT)
- ■ ICING (CONFECTIONERS') SUGAR
- ■ SALT
- ■ OLIVE OIL
- ◆

PREPARATION TIME: 30 MINUTES

SEPARATE OUT THE EGGS and beat the yolks with a fork, adding a pinch of salt. Whisk the egg whites until stiff and fold slowly into the beaten yolks. Place a large frying pan with a little oil over gentle heat and pour in the beaten eggs. Using a pallet knife or spatula, push a part of the egg towards the opposite end of the pan. Spread a spoonful of marmalade or jam over the thin layer which has already set and fold over a flap of the omelette to cover it. With the aid of the pallet knife, gradually roll the omelette up, adding the marmalade or jam as you go. In this way, you will have a Swiss Roll-type omelette. Place it on a serving dish, dredge with icing sugar and cut into slices.

FRITTELLA
SMOTHERED ARTICHOKES, BROAD BEANS AND PEAS

- ◆
- ■ 4 GLOBE ARTICHOKES
- ■ 300 G / ¾ LB SHELLED PEAS
- ■ 300 G / ¾ LB FRESH, HULLED BROAD BEANS
- ■ 1 SMALL ONION
- ■ SALT
- ■ PEPPER
- ■ OLIVE OIL
- ◆

PREPARATION TIME: 45 MINUTES

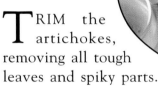

TRIM the artichokes, removing all tough leaves and spiky parts. Slice. Brown the chopped onion in a little oil and add the artichokes, peas and broad beans to the pan (preferably one in earthenware). Season with salt and pepper and cover with a lid. Simmer over gentle heat for about 30 minutes, stirring from time to time. Should the vegetables dry out, add a glass of warm water. This is a very ancient dish, typical especially of the Palermo area. The origin of the name is not clear. Some scholars believe that there is a Latin origin to the name ("frigere") because the ingredients are put all together with the oil in a roomy pan, but without the addition of water.

VARIATION: add a glass or half a cup of vinegar before drawing off the heat.

GAMBERETTI AL LIMONE

PRAWNS IN LEMON

◆

- 500 G / 1 LB / VERY FRESH, UNCOOKED PRAWNS (SHRIMPS)
- 2-3 LEMONS
- 25 G / 1 OZ / 2 TBSP SALTED CAPERS
- 5-6 MINT LEAVES
- OLIVE OIL, SALT AND PEPPER

◆

PREPARATION TIME: 1 HOUR

SHELL THE UNCOOKED PRAWNS and arrange in a bowl. Squeeze the lemons and pour the juice over the prawns. Season with salt and pepper.

In the meantime, soak the capers so as to eliminate the salt. Drain well and transfer to the bowl with a leaf of mint to lend aroma. Dress with oil.

Leave to macerate, stirring from time to time.

A PIECE OF ADVICE: try getting this dish ready in advance - in the morning, for example, when it is to be relished in the evening. In this way, the prawns will be more flavoursome.

INSALATA CON POLPO BOLLITO
BOILED OCTOPUS SALAD

B OIL THE OCTOPUS IN SALTED WATER. When cooked, cut it into pieces and dress with olive oil, salt and lemon to taste.

To help you cook the octopus well without it becoming tough, here is a suggestion from a fisherman: put a wine cork in with the cooking water.

The effect of the cork on the octopus has no scientific explanation, but I can assure you that it *does* work.

- 1 KG / 2 LBS OCTOPUS
- JUICE FROM 1 LEMON
- OLIVE OIL AND SALT

◆

PREPARATION TIME: 1 HOUR

INSALATA DI MARE
SEA FOOD SALAD

- 500 G / 1 LB BABY CLAMS IN THEIR SHELLS
- 500 G / 1 LB MUSSELS IN THEIR SHELLS
- 1 CLOVE OF GARLIC
- 1 LEMON
- PINCH OF OREGANO
- HOT RED PEPPERS

PREPARATION TIME: 2 HOURS

WASH THE BABY CLAMS and the mussels in running water. Cook the sea food in water in a saucepan until they open up. Take them out of their shells, season with olive oil, lemon juice, oregano and hot red pepper. Leave to steep for a few hours before serving at table.

———————————

VARIATION: another type of sea food salad is the "fantasia di mare", which is richer in fish, but just as simple.

Boil the fish, remove them from their shells and dress with chopped garlic and parsley, salt, pepper or hot red pepper and lemon juice.

Ingredients:
4-5 SMALL OCTOPUSES
200 G / 8 OZ BABY SQUID
200 G / 8 OZ BABY CUTTLEFISH
200 G / 8 OZ CLAM-LIKE LIMPETS
200 G / 8 OZ MUSSELS
1 CLOVE OF GARLIC
2 LEMONS
BUNCH OF PARSLEY
OLIVE OIL AND SALT, PEPPER OR HOT RED PEPPER

INSALATA ESTIVA
SUMMER SALAD

- 2 BOILED POTATOES
- 200 G / 8 OZ BOILED GREEN (RUNNER) BEANS
- 2-3 SALAD TOMATOES
- 1 LARGE BAKED ONION

PREPARATION TIME: 1 HOUR

CUT THE POTATOES, tomatoes and the green beans into chunks and slice the onion. Season with olive oil, salt and pepper.
This dish can be enriched with hard-boiled eggs and tuna fish, making it into a one-course meal.
It is the salad par excellence, especially in Palermo, where greengrocers often sell ready-cooked vegetables.

———————————

VARIATION: seasoned green olives, pickles, chunks of fresh cheese (primosale or a mild pro- vola) may be added to the classi- cal salad together with left-overs of boiled meat, if you have any.

INSALATA FANTASIA DI ARANCE
ORANGE SALAD

- 2 LARGE ORANGES
- SALT
- PEPPER
- OLIVE OIL

PREPARATION TIME: 30 MINUTES

YOU MAY USE two different qualities of oranges for this salad: blood oranges with their red pulp, or the Portuguese ones with their yellow pulp.

Peel the fruit and cut into chunks, dress with oil, salt and pepper. The dish can be enriched with pieces of anchovy or herring and black olives or onion.

Considered an excellent appetiser, this salad stimulates the secretion of gastric juices which prepares the stomach to digest the meal.

VARIATION: you may use lemons instead of oranges. Dress with parsley, chopped garlic, olive oil, salt and pepper.

LUMACHE CON AGLIO E PREZZEMOLO
SNAILS WITH PARSLEY AND GARLIC

- 1 KG / 2 LBS SNAILS IN THEIR SHELLS
- 3 CLOVES OF GARLIC
- 1 SPRIG OF PARSLEY
- PINCH OF CINNAMON
- OLIVE OIL AND SALT
- PEPPER

PREPARATION TIME: 1 HOUR

IN A POT (preferably an earthenware one), brown the chopped cloves of garlic in plenty of oil, together with the snails, the parsley, salt, pepper and a pinch of cinnamon.
Stir well to allow the flavours to blend and simmer gently for 20 minutes over low heat.
This dish is a feature of the feast day of Palermo's patron saint, Santa Rosalia.

THE SNAILS MARKED OUT for this recipe are the white snails called crastuna because of the long horns which bring to mind "u crastu" (castrated lamb).
They are gathered off the leaves of herbaceous plants after the first summer rains.

LUMACHE IN SALSA
SNAILS IN TOMATO SAUCE

- 1 KG / 2 LBS SNAILS
- 1 CHOPPED ONION
- 1 KG / 2 LBS RIPE TOMATOES
- SALT
- PEPPER
- OLIVE OIL

PREPARATION TIME: 1 HOUR

BROWN THE ONION in a little oil in a saucepan. When golden, add the skinned tomatoes, roughly chopped and deprived of their seeds. Season with salt and pepper.
Stir, mashing the tomatoes with a fork, throw in the snails and cook for 20 minutes.

BLACK SNAILS ARE USED FOR THIS RECIPE. They are called "attuppateddi", signifying that their shells are sealed with a membrane. These are the typical dishes for the feast of Palermo's patron saint, Santa Rosalia, celebrated between the end of June and the beginning of July.
"Ziti a vasari e babbaluci a sucari su così chi nun ponnu mai saziari".
(Kissing between courting couples and sucking on snails / are things which never satiate).
E. Alaimo "Proverbi siciliani"
Edit. Martello.

MELANZANE ALLA PARMIGIANA
AUBERGINE / EGGPLANT PIE

- 5 AUBERGINES (EGGPLANTS)
- 1 KG / 2 LBS TOMATOES
- 500 G / 1 LB ONIONS
- 150 G / 6 OZ PRIMOSALE CHEESE
- 100 G / 4 OZ / 1 CUP GRATED CHEESE
- BASIL
- SALT
- PEPPER
- OIL FOR FRYING

PREPARATION TIME: 2 HOURS

PEEL AND SLICE THE AUBERGINES and soak in salted water for about 30 minutes. Drain, rinse, dry and fry in very hot oil.

In the meanwhile, make some tomato sauce with plenty of basil. Put a layer of aubergine in the bottom of an oiled baking pan, cover with the tomato sauce, sprinkle grated cheese over and arrange a few slices of the primosale on top. Continue with more layers of aubergine, dressed as previously, until all the ingredients have been used up.

The final layer will consist of aubergine and grated cheese. Drizzle a little olive oil over and bake in a hot oven for about 15 minutes.

VARIATION: peel the aubergines, slice and soak in salted water for about thirty minutes.

Drain, rinse, dry and place on a scalding hotplate (griddle). Season in the same way as in the recipe above. The vegetable becomes more digestible in this way, and is just as tasty.

MELANZANE IN COTOLETTA

BREADED AUBERGINES / EGGPLANTS

◆

- 3 ROUND AUBERGINES (EGGPLANTS)
- 100 G / 4 OZ / 1 CUP DRY BREADCRUMBS
- 50 G / 2 OZ / ⅓ CUP FLOUR
- 2 EGGS
- OIL FOR FRYING

◆

PREPARATION TIME: 2½ HOURS

WITHOUT PEELING, cut the large, round aubergines into slices ½ inch thick and place in a roomy bowl with salted water for a couple of hours. Remove the slices from the water, squeeze and toss in the flour, the beaten egg and then the dry breadcrumbs. Fry in scalding oil and serve.

MELANZANE IN SFORMATO

AUBERGINE OR EGGPLANT PUDDING

◆

- 5 AUBERGINES (EGGPLANTS)
- 100 G / 4 OZ / 1 CUP DRY BREADCRUMBS
- 50 G / 2 OZ / ½ CUP GRATED CHEESE
- 1 EGG
- 50 G / 2 OZ CACIOCAVALLO OR SMOKED PROVOLA OR OTHER STRONG-FLAVOURED CHEESE
- 50 G / 2 OZ MORTADELLA OR SALAMI SAUSAGE
- CHOPPED MINT
- CHOPPED BASIL

◆

PREPARATION TIME: 1 HOUR

BOIL THE AUBERGINES in salted water, drain and allow to cool in a colander. Squeeze when completely cool to remove most of the cooking water. Transfer the vegetable to a bowl, add most of the dry breadcrumbs, the grated cheese, the whole egg and the chopped basil and mint.

Should the mixture be too soggy, add more breadcrumbs to make it thicker.

Mix well to blend the flavours and turn half the mixture into an oiled-and-crumbed baking dish.

Arrange the salami and caciocavallo slices on top and cover with the other half of the mixture.

Bake in a hot oven for about 20 minutes.

MELANZANE IN POLPETTE
AUBERGINE OLIVES

◆

- 4 AUBERGINES (EGGPLANTS)
- 100 G / 4 OZ / 1 CUP DRY BREADCRUMBS
- 50 G / 2 OZ / ½ CUP GRATED CHEESE
- 3 EGGS
- 50 G / 2 OZ SALAMI SAUSAGE
- 50 G / 2 OZ CACIOCAVALLO CHEESE
- CHOPPED BASIL
- CHOPPED MINT

◆

PREPARATION TIME: 1 HOUR

BOIL THE AUBERGINES in salted water, drain them and allow to rest in a colander. Squeeze them when really cool to remove most of the cooking water. Transfer the aubergine to a bowl, add most of the breadcrumbs, the grated cheese, an egg and the chopped basil and mint. Mix well and throw in the diced salami and caciocavallo.

Roll into oval-shaped balls and dip into the egg which has been beaten up with the breadcrumbs. Fry in scalding oil.

MELANZANE IN SALSA AGRODOLCE
AUBERGINES IN A SWEET AND SOUR SAUCE

◆

- 4 SWEET (BELL) PEPPERS
- 4 AUBERGINES (EGGPLANTS)
- 1 KG / 2 LBS POTATOES
- 500 G / 1 LB ONIONS
- 125 ML / 4 FL OZ / 8 TBSP WHITE VINEGAR
- 1 TBSP GRANULATED SUGAR
- OIL FOR FRYING

◆

PREPARATION TIME: 1½ HOURS

CUT THE AUBERGINES into small pieces and place in a bowl of salted water for about 2 hours.

Clean the sweet peppers and cut into strips. Peel and cut the potatoes into chunks. Finely slice the onions. Fry the potatoes in scalding oil in a large frying pan. Season with salt before drawing off the heat.

In the same oil, fry the sweet peppers and then the squeezed aubergine. Last of all, add the onions. Pour off any excess oil and return to the heat with the aubergine, the sweet peppers, the potatoes and the onions. Mix, sprinkle with sugar, spray with the white vinegar and put on the lid.

Turn off the heat and leave to rest for 15 minutes before mixing and serving.

MELANZANE IN INVOLTINO
AUBERGINE BUNDLES

- 4 AUBERGINES (EGGPLANTS)
- 3 HARD-BOILED EGGS
- 100 G / 4 OZ FRESH CACIOCAVALLO OR MILD PROVOLA CHEESE
- 100 G / 4 OZ SALAMI
- 50 G / 2 OZ / ½ CUP GRATED CHEESE
- 2 SOUP LADLES / 8 TBSP HOME-MADE TOMATO SAUCE
- A FEW MINT LEAVES
- SALT
- OLIVE OIL

PREPARATION TIME: 2 HOURS

PEEL AND SLICE THE AUBERGINES. Arrange in a bowl of salted water for about an hour, so that they lose their bitter flavour.

Take out of the water, dry on kitchen paper and fry in hot oil. In a bowl, mix the boiled eggs and the diced cheese and salami. Spread a little of the mixture on each aubergine slice, roll up and place in an oiled baking pan. Make a layer of bundles which you will cover with the tomato sauce. Dredge with grated cheese and mint, dress with a trickle of olive oil and bake in a hot oven for 10 minutes.

VARIATION: if you wish to make the dish more digestible but just as flavoursome, try cooking the aubergines on a searing hotplate (griddle). In this way, you avoid frying them.

MELANZANE SOTT'OLIO
AUBERGINES IN OIL

- 5 AUBERGINES (EGGPLANTS)
- 4 CLOVES OF GARLIC CUT INTO PIECES
- OREGANO
- BASIL
- MINT
- VINEGAR
- HOT RED PEPPERS
- OLIVE OIL

PREPARATION TIME: 2 HOURS

SLICE THE AUBERGINES and soak in salted water for about an hour. Rinse, dry and place the slices on a searing hotplate (griddle) or in a heated iron frying pan. Arrange the grilled slices in layers in a jar or bowl. Season each layer with the garlic pieces, a pinch of oregano, a few mint and basil leaves and some hot red pepper. Pour the oil and a little vinegar over to cover the aubergine slices. Repeat until all the ingredients have been used up.

VARIATION: after soaking the aubergines in salted water, take them out and put to boil in a saucepan with 1 part water and 2 parts vinegar for 10 minutes. Drain, dry well and season with the same ingredients as in the above recipe.

MELANZANE RIPIENE
STUFFED AUBERGINES / EGGPLANTS

◆

- ■ 3 AUBERGINES (EGGPLANTS)
- ■ 4 CLOVES OF GARLIC
- ■ 4-5 RIPE TOMATOES
- ■ 100 G / 4 OZ / ¼ LB CACIOCAVALLO OR A SHARP PROVOLA CHEESE
- ■ 50 G / 2 OZ / ½ CUP GRATED CHEESE
- ■ 4 OR 5 BASIL LEAVES
- ■ SALT
- ■ PEPPER

◆

PREPARATION TIME: 1 HOUR

CUT THE AUBERGINES LENGTHWAYS. With the tip of a sharp knife, make several slits in the flesh of the vegetable and scald in salted water for 10 minutes.

Place the cut side face down on a napkin or a kitchen paper towel to drain.

Dry and allow to cool. Cut the garlic and the caciocavallo into pieces and insert into the slits. Aromatise with some basil and cover each aubergine slice with the tomato sauce which you will have prepared as follows: gently fry two whole cloves of garlic (to be subsequently removed) in a little olive oil; chop up 4 or 5 ripe tomatoes, skinned and with their seeds discarded; cook for 5 to 10 minutes, stirring; add salt and pepper and aromatise with chopped basil. Mask the aubergines with the sauce, dust with the grated cheese, drizzle over some oil and bake for 30 minutes in a hot oven at 180° C/350° F/Gas mark 4.

MELANZANE RIPIENE DI CARNE

MEAT-STUFFED AUBERGINES / EGGPLANTS

- 3 AUBERGINES (EGGPLANTS)
- 250 G / 8 OZ MINCED (GROUND) MEAT
- 50 G / 2 OZ / ½ CUP DRY BREADCRUMBS
- 50 G / 2 OZ / ½ CUP GRATED CHEESE
- 50 G / 2 OZ / ¼ CUP CAPERS
- 50 G / 2 OZ PRIMOSALE CHEESE OR ANOTHER FRESH CHEESE
- 50 G / 2 OZ / ⅓ CUP STONED GREEN OLIVES
- 3-4 BASIL LEAVES
- 3 RIPE TOMATOES
- 2 CLOVES OF GARLIC
- 2 SMALL ONIONS
- 1 EGG
- OREGANO
- SALT AND PEPPER

PREPARATION TIME: 1½ HOURS

CUT THE AUBERGINES LENGTHWAYS. With the tip of a sharp knife, make several slits in the flesh of the vegetable. Grease a baking pan with oil flavoured with a pinch of oregano, and arrange the aubergines in it with the cut side face down. Bake in a hot oven for 10 minutes, take out and leave to cool. Scrape the flesh from the skins, hollowing them out to make shell cases. Put the capers in hot water to draw out the salt. In a bowl, mix together the minced meat, egg, grated cheese, salt and pepper. Drain the capers and chop up with the onions, olives and basil.

Add to the meat and mix thoroughly until evenly amalgamated. Distribute the mixture among the aubergine shells. Cover each with a slice of primosale or another type of fresh cheese and a few pieces of tomato. Sprinkle with dry breadcrumbs, season with a trickle of olive oil and bake in a hot oven for about 30 minutes.

OLIVE CONDITE
DRESSED OLIVES

- 500 G / 1 LB / 3 CUPS GREEN OLIVES
- 2 CLOVES OF GARLIC
- BASIL
- PARSLEY
- HOT RED PEPPERS
- OLIVE OIL
- VINEGAR

PREPARATION TIME: 2 HOURS

CRUSH THE OLIVES and season with the garlic, basil, parsley and hot red peppers, all chopped up together. Fill the jar with olive oil to cover and a few drops of vinegar.

VARIATIONS: the olives can be flavoured with pickles, or else with oregano and garlic covered in oil, or even with a brine solution - 1 l (2 pints / 4 cups) water and 200 g (8 oz / ⅔ cup) salt.

This dish goes very well with a salad of tender Florence fennel and/or tomatoes. It is never lacking from the Sicilian larder in any season of the year so unexpected guests can always be offered an "aperitivo".

OLIVE CON PANGRATTATO FRITTO
FRIED BREADED OLIVES

- **500 G / 1 LB / 3 CUPS GREEN OLIVES**
- **100 G / 4 OZ / 1 CUP DRY BREADCRUMBS**
- **1 CLOVE OF GARLIC**
- **HOT RED PEPPER**
- **OLIVE OIL**
- **VINEGAR**

PREPARATION TIME: 2½ HOURS

BROWN THE BREADCRUMBS in a little oil in a frying pan, stirring continuously. Score the olives, put them in a bowl and season with chopped parsley and garlic.
Add the hot red pepper, olive oil, a squirt of vinegar and the dry breadcrumbs. Mix well and serve.

THIS IS AN EASY appetiser to prepare because, in the Sicilian larder, there is never a lack of olives in brine, dry breadcrumbs, garlic, olive oil and hot red peppers. It is an excellent dish to serve with wine.

PANELLE
FLAT CHICKPEA LOAVES

- **500 G / 1 LB / 3 CUPS CHICKPEA (GARBANZO) FLOUR**
- **WATER**
- **SALT**

PREPARATION TIME: 30 MINUTES

BRING A SAUCEPAN WITH SALTED WATER TO BOIL. When it starts to bubble, sprinkle in the chickpea flour. Keep mixing with a wooden spoon until a rather thick paste forms. Pour onto a pastry board and, with the aid of a pallet knife or spatula, spread it out to make a very thin layer. Then, using the rim of a glass, cut out little, round, flat loaves and fry in hot oil.

CROCCHETTE DI PATATE
POTATO CROQUETTES

- 1 KG / 2 LBS POTATOES
- 3 EGGS
- 50 G / 2 OZ / ½ CUP GRATED CHEESE
- 100 G / 4 OZ / 1 CUP DRY BREADCRUMBS
- CHOPPED PARSLEY

PREPARATION TIME: 2 HOURS

BOIL THE POTATOES in salted water. Peel and put through a vegetable mill to make a purée. Season with the grated cheese, the dry breadcrumbs, the chopped parsley, salt, pepper and the 3 egg yolks. Pour the egg whites into a bowl and put the dry breadcrumbs into another. Mix the purée well and form little fingers.

Dip these into the egg whites (whisked up with a fork) and then the breadcrumbs. Deep fry in hot oil.

CROCCHETTE DI PATATE CON CARNE
POTATO CROQUETTES WITH MEAT

- 1 KG / 2 LBS POTATOES
- 4 EGGS
- 50 G / 2 OZ / ½ CUP GRATED CHEESE
- 100 G / 4 OZ / 1 CUP DRY BREADCRUMBS
- 300 G / ¾ LB MINCED (GROUND) MEAT
- 1 MEDIUM-SIZED ONION
- 125 ML / 4 FL OZ / 8 TBSP WHITE WINE
- HOME-MADE TOMATO
- SAUCE
- CHOPPED PARSLEY

PREPARATION TIME: 2 HOURS

BOIL THE POTATOES in salted water, peel and put through a vegetable mill to mash them.

Season with half the grated cheese and dry breadcrumbs, the parsley, salt, pepper and two egg yolks. Keep the egg whites aside in a bowl. Boil the other eggs until hard. Sauté the chopped onion in a little oil until golden, add the minced meat and the white wine. After a few minutes, add the tomato purée and cook until the meat sauce is dense. Add the grated cheese and the roughly-chopped, hard-boiled eggs to the meat. Make cups with the potato mixture, filling them with a spoonful of the meat sauce.

Cover with the remaining potato mixture to form croquettes which you will dip into the whisked egg whites and then into the dry breadcrumbs. Deep fry in hot oil.

PATATE AL FORNO
POTATOES AU GRATIN

◆

- ■ 1 KG / 2 LBS POTATOES
- ■ 500 G / 1 LB ONIONS
- ■ 4 RIPE TOMATOES
- ■ A FEW PIECES OF CHEESE AND/OR SALAMI SAUSAGE

◆

PREPARATION TIME: 1 HOUR

PEEL THE POTATOES, wash and slice. Oil a baking dish and arrange a layer of potato slices on the bottom. Scatter over a little finely-sliced onion, pieces of cheese and/or salami, and pieces of skinned and seeded tomatoes. Continue layering the ingredients until they are all used up. The last layer will be of tomatoes and basil. Trickle a little olive oil over the top and bake in a hot oven for about 45 minutes.

This makes an excellent accompaniment to meat or cheese served up for supper.

PATATE E RICOTTA IN POLPETTE
POTATO AND RICOTTA CHEESE PATTIES

◆

- 1 KG / 2 LBS POTATOES (THE OLDER THE BETTER)
- 100 G / 4 OZ / 1 CUP GRATED CHEESE
- 100 G / 4 OZ / 1 CUP DRY BREADCRUMBS
- 4 EGGS
- 500 G / 1 LB RICOTTA
- CHOPPED PARSLEY
- NUTMEG
- SALT
- PEPPER
- OIL FOR FRYING

◆

PREPARATION TIME: 1½ HOURS

BOIL THE POTATOES, peel and mash them in a vegetable mill.
Add two eggs, the grated cheese, salt, pepper, chopped parsley and a handful of dry breadcrumbs to thicken the mixture. Mix to amalgamate the ingredients thoroughly. In a bowl, mash the ricotta with a fork, season with salt and a little ground nutmeg. Make little nests with the mixture in your palms, dampened with water, and fill up the hollows with a spoonful of ricotta, sealing with more of the potato mixture to form a ball. Dip each patty first into the beaten egg and then into the breadcrumbs.
Deep fry in hot oil. This dish is typical of spring when ricotta is at its best.

PATATE IN TORTA
POTATO CAKE

- 1 KG / 2 LBS POTATOES
- 1 EGG
- 50 G / 2 OZ / ½ CUP GRATED CHEESE
- 100 G / 4 OZ FRESH CHEESE (PRIMOSALE, CACIOCAVALLO OR PROVOLA)
- 50 G / 2 OZ SALAMI OR
- MORTADELLA
- 50 G / 2 OZ / ½ CUP DRY BREADCRUMBS
- PARSLEY
- BASIL

PREPARATION TIME: 1 HOUR

BOIL THE POTATOES in salted water, peel and put through a vegetable mill to mash them.
Season with the grated cheese, parsley, basil, egg, salt and pepper. If the mixture is too soft, add a handful or so of breadcrumbs.
Oil a baking pan and sprinkle a layer of breadcrumbs over it. Spread half the potato mixture over the bottom of the dish. Arrange the salami and cheese slices on top and cover with the rest of the mash. Bake in a hot oven for about 30 minutes until a crust forms.

VARIATION: various ingredients may be used for the filling. You may use up left-over meat stew, sausages, ricotta cheese, meat sauce left over from a pasta dish and minced with peas, etc.....

PEPERONI ARROSTITI
ROAST SWEET PEPPERS

- 8 SWEET (BELL) PEPPERS
- 4 CLOVES OF GARLIC
- 3 ANCHOVY FILLETS
- 1 LEMON
- CHOPPED BASIL
- SALT
- PEPPER OR HOT RED PEPPER
- OLIVE OIL

PREPARATION TIME: 2 HOURS

BAKE THE PEPPERS in a hot oven until they wrinkle and wilt. Take them out and allow to cool. Discard the stalk, eliminate the seeds completely and peel.

Cut the peppers into strips and arrange them in a bowl into which you will have poured a little olive oil. Crush the anchovy fillets separately with a fork and add. Season the whole lot with the chopped basil and garlic and the lemon juice. Hot red pepper may be added if you wish.

This is an excellent antipasto which can be prepared during the summer and kept in the larder for two or three months.

PEPERONI RIPIENI DI CARNE

MEAT-STUFFED SWEET PEPPERS

◆

- 6 SWEET (BELL) PEPPERS
- 300 G / ¾ LB MINCED (GROUND) MEAT
- 80 G / 3 OZ / ¾ CUP GRATED CHEESE
- 50 G / 2 OZ / ½ CUP DRY BREADCRUMBS
- 2-3 CHOPPED BASIL LEAVES SPRIG OF PARSLEY
- 1 EGG
- 1 SOUP LADLE / 4 TBSP HOME-MADE TOMATO SAUCE

◆

PREPARATION TIME: 45 MINUTES

WASH THE PEPPERS, dry, and remove the stalk. Mix the minced meat in a bowl with the egg, the grated cheese, the dry breadcrumbs and the chopped parsley and basil. If the mixture is not soft enough, add a little tomato purée. Stuff the peppers and arrange them upright in an ovenproof dish with a little water and olive oil to cover the bottom. Bake in a hot oven for about thirty minutes. Serve hot.

PEPERONI RIPIENI ALLA PALERMITANA
STUFFED PEPPERS, PALERMO-STYLE

◆

- 6 SWEET (BELL) PEPPERS
- 150 G / 6 OZ / 1½ CUPS DRY BREADCRUMBS
- 3 ANCHOVY FILLETS
- 100 G / 4 OZ / 1 CUP GRATED PECORINO CHEESE
- 1 SOUP LADLE / 4 TBSP HOME-MADE TOMATO SAUCE
- 30 G / 1 OZ / 3 TBSP SULTANAS OR RAISINS
- 30 G / 1 OZ / 4 TBSP PINE NUTS
- 150 G / 6 OZ DICED CACIOCAVALLO OR SPICY PROVOLA CHEESE
- 100G / 4 OZ SALAMI, CUT INTO PIECES

◆

PREPARATION TIME: 1½ HOURS

REMOVE THE PEPPER STALKS and discard the seeds. Put the oil and the anchovy fillets (crushing them with a fork) in a frying pan. Add the dry breadcrumbs, the sultanas and pine nuts and gently fry everything, continuously mixing so that lumps do not form. Cool and add the grated cheese, the diced cheese and the salami. Pour in a soup ladle of tomato purée to blend everything together.

Stuff the peppers with the mixture and arrange in a baking dish with a little water and oil so that they do not stick to the bottom. Bake for about 30 minutes in a hot oven.

PEPERONATA
PEPPER RAGOUT

◆

- 1 KG / 2 LBS SWEET (BELL)
- PEPPERS
- 2 CLOVES OF GARLIC
- 4 ANCHOVY FILLETS
- 50 G / 2 OZ / 4 TBSP PICKLED CAPERS
- 500 G / 1 LB TOMATOES
- BASIL
- OLIVE OIL

◆

PREPARATION TIME: 45 MINUTES

PUT A LITTLE OLIVE OIL, the chopped garlic and the anchovies, crushed with a fork, in a saucepan. Remove the seeds from the peppers, shred and place in the pan. Cover with the lid and simmer for 15 minutes. Add the capers, the roughly-chopped, seeded tomatoes and the basil. Cook for a further 15 minutes.

POMODORI SECCATI SOTT'OLIO
DRIED TOMATOES IN OIL

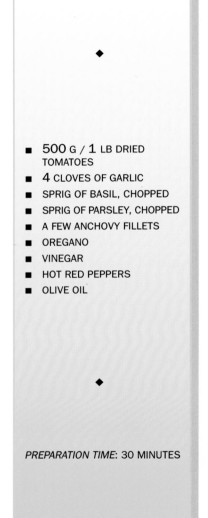

- 500 G / 1 LB DRIED TOMATOES
- 4 CLOVES OF GARLIC
- SPRIG OF BASIL, CHOPPED
- SPRIG OF PARSLEY, CHOPPED
- A FEW ANCHOVY FILLETS
- OREGANO
- VINEGAR
- HOT RED PEPPERS
- OLIVE OIL

PREPARATION TIME: 30 MINUTES

BLANCH THE TOMATOES very briefly in a solution of 1 part vinegar to 3 parts water (1 or 2 minutes will be enough). Dry well on kitchen paper. Arrange a layer of tomatoes in a bowl and dress with pieces of garlic, a pinch of chopped basil and parsley and hot red peppers. Cover with olive oil and a few drops of vinegar. Repeat the layers, finishing with the oil in which the anchovies have been dissolved.

POMODORI SFIZIOSI ALLA PALERMITANA
PALERMO-STYLE TOMATOES

- 6 LARGE TOMATOES
- 150 G / 6 OZ / 1½ CUPS DRY BREADCRUMBS
- 30 G / 1 OZ / 2 TBSP CAPERS
- 30 G / 1 OZ / 3 TBSP PITTED (STONED) GREEN OLIVES
- 4 ANCHOVY FILLETS
- BASIL
- PARSLEY
- SALT
- PEPPER
- OLIVE OIL

PREPARATION TIME: 2½ HOURS

UOVA E PISELLI
EGGS WITH PEAS

- 6 EGGS
- 500 G / 1 LB PEAS
- 2 SMALL ONIONS
- SALT
- PEPPER
- OLIVE OIL

PREPARATION TIME: 30 MINUTES

WASH THE TOMATOES, dry and scoop the flesh out into a bowl. Cover the bottom of a frying pan with a little olive oil and the anchovies, crushed with a fork. Add the dry breadcrumbs and, stirring continuously, leave to brown. Turn them into the bowl of tomato pulp, add the chopped parsley and basil and a little oil. Mix well and distribute the mixture among the tomato cases. Arrange in an ovenproof dish and pop into a moderate oven.

BROWN THE CHOPPED ONION in a saucepan, throw in the peas, season with salt and pepper and add water to cover. Cook for about 15 minutes. Break in the eggs, cover with the lid and lower the flame. When the eggs are veiled in white, draw off the heat and serve.

This is a spring dish when the peas are still small and sweet. They are usually in copious supply and are also used as a sauce for spaghetti.

UOVA SODE IN SALSA DI POMODORO
HARD-BOILED EGGS IN TOMATO SAUCE

- 5 EGGS
- 2 SOUP LADLES / 8 TBSP HOME-MADE TOMATO SAUCE
- 50 G / 2 OZ / ½ CUP DRY BREADCRUMBS
- SALT AND PEPPER
- OLIVE OIL

PREPARATION TIME: 30 MINUTES

BOIL FOUR OF THE EGGS in salted water until hard. Shell, and cut lengthways.

Beat the remaining egg with a fork and plunge each half of the hard-boiled eggs first in the beaten egg and then in the breadcrumbs. Fry in hot oil and embed in the sauce. Cook for five minutes before serving.

THIS DISH was a main course in the daily fare of the common people. As with almost all main course dishes, the sauce can also be exploited served up with pasta for a first course.

UOVA ROTTE NEL SUGO
EGGS POACHED IN TOMATO SAUCE

- ■ 4-5 EGGS
- ■ HOME-MADE TOMATO SAUCE
- ■ SALT
- ■ PEPPER

PREPARATION TIME: 15 MINUTES

HEAT UP THE HOME-MADE TOMATO SAUCE in a wide pan and, when it is nice and hot, break the eggs into the pan, one at a time. Put on the lid.

The eggs will encase themselves in their whites after 2 or 3 minutes. Draw off the heat, remove the eggs with a palette knife and arrange on a serving plate.

UOVA SODE RIPIENE
STUFFED HARD-BOILED EGGS

- ■ 6 HARD-BOILED EGGS
- ■ 200 G / 8 OZ / 1 CUP TUNA FISH IN OIL
- ■ 2 PICKLED GHERKINS
- ■ 30 G / 1 OZ / 2 TBSP PICKLED CAPERS
- ■ 2 CHOPPED SHALLOTS (SCALLIONS)
- ■ 1 SPRIG PARSLEY, CHOPPED
- ■ 1 TBSP MAYONNAISE

PREPARATION TIME: 45 MINUTES

CHOP UP THE TUNA FISH, onion, gherkins and capers in a grinder.

Cut the hard-boiled eggs lengthways, scoop out the yolks and put them in a bowl, together with the tuna and onion.

Blend everything well with a fork, add the parsley and bind with a spoonful of mayonnaise.

Fill the egg whites with the mixture. Arrange on a serving dish, garnish with parsley sprigs and serve.

UOVA STRAPAZZATE CON IL PANE FRITTO
SCRAMBLED EGGS WITH FRIED BREAD

- ■ 4-5 EGGS
- ■ 2-3 SLICES STALE BREAD
- ■ 125 ML / 4 FL OZ / 8 TBSP MILK
- ■ SALT
- ■ PEPPER
- ■ OLIVE OIL

PREPARATION TIME: 20 MINUTES

MOISTEN THE BREAD SLICES IN THE MILK, then cut into cubes. Heat the oil in a frying pan to fry the bread in. Pour the eggs over and mix well with the bread until cooked.

Season with salt and pepper and serve.

THIS DISH used to be served as the main course after soup or pasta in the homes of shepherds, miners and peasants. In baronial abodes, on the other hand, it was served up as an appetiser or to accompany boiled and roasted fish and meat. Such a dish is served up for breakfast, however, in France and England.

FIORI DI ZUCCA FRITTI IN PASTELLA
COURGETTE FLOWER FRITTERS

- ■ 500 G / 1 LB COURGETTE (ZUCCHINI) FLOWERS
- ■ 150 G / 6 OZ / 1 CUP WHITE FLOUR
- ■ ¼ TSP FRESH BREWER'S YEAST
- ■ MILK
- ■ SALT
- ■ PEPPER
- ■ OIL FOR FRYING

PREPARATION TIME: 40 MINUTES

BLANCH THE MARROW FLOWERS in salted water for 5 minutes and drain well. Meanwhile prepare a batter with the flour and brewer's yeast dissolved in the warm milk, along with salt and pepper.

Dip the courgette flowers into the batter. Heat some oil in a frying pan and when nice and hot, pick up the flowers-in-batter in a spoon and drop into the oil. Fry until golden.

VARIATION: the batter can be made differently. Mix the warm water into the flour with a pinch of brewer's yeast, an egg (previously beaten with a fork) and pieces of anchovy. Leave to rest for about 30 minutes before coating the flowers and frying them.

ZUCCA ALL'AGRODOLCE

SWEET AND SOUR PUMPKIN

- 1 KG / 2 LBS PUMPKIN (SQUASH)
- 1 CLOVE OF GARLIC
- 125 ML / 8 TBSP VINEGAR
- 1 TBSP GRANULATED SUGAR
- PINCH OF CINNAMON
- A FEW MINT LEAVES
- OLIVE OIL

PREPARATION TIME: 1 HOUR

CUT THE PUMPKIN into slices roughly ½ in thick and fry in hot oil with the whole clove of garlic which you will discard as soon as it colours. When all the slices are fried, put them back all together in the pan, draining off the superfluous oil. Dredge with sugar, chopped mint and cinnamon. Mix with care, pour the vinegar over, cover with the lid and turn off the heat.

SICILIAN PUMPKIN (squash) and courgette (zucchini) recipes are rather scarce. The reason is that this vegetable is considered to be insipid. There is a proverb which goes "Sali mitticinni nà visazza / conzala come vuoi è sempre cucuzza". (Add a lot of salt and seasoning because pumpkin it always remains.)

ZUCCHINE FRITTE IN AGRODOLCE

FRIED COURGETTES WITH A SWEET AND SOUR SAUCE

◆

- 1 KG / 2 LBS COURGETTES (ZUCCHINI)
- 125 ML / 4 FL OZ / 8 TBSP VINEGAR
- 1 TSP GRANULATED SUGAR
- 4-5 MINT LEAVES
- 30 G / 1 OZ / 3 TBSP SULTANAS OR RAISINS
- 1 CLOVE OF GARLIC

◆

PREPARATION TIME: 30 MINUTES

SCRAPE THE COURGETTES and slice into rounds. Fry in very hot oil where you will have put the whole clove of garlic, to be removed as soon as it colours. When all the courgettes are fried, put them back into the frying pan and sprinkle with the sugar, chopped mint and sultanas.

Mix carefully and pour over a glass of vinegar. Cover and turn off the heat.

––––––––––––

VARIATION: if you add 4/5 beaten eggs with salt and pepper and a pinch of parsley to the fried courgettes, you will obtain an excellent omelette to be cooked in a pan with very little oil.

ZUCCHINE RIPIENE
STUFFED COURGETTES

◆

- 1 KG / 2 LBS COURGETTES (ZUCCHINI)
- 300 G / ¾ LB MINCED (GROUND) MEAT
- 1 MEDIUM-SIZED ONION
- 30 G / 1 OZ / 2 TBSP CAPERS
- 50 G / 2 OZ / ⅓ CUP GREEN OLIVES
- A FEW TABLESPOONS HOME-MADE TOMATO SAUCE
- BASIL
- SALT
- OLIVE OIL

◆

PREPARATION TIME: 1 HOUR

B LANCH THE COURGETTES for 10 minutes. Drain, allow to cool and cut lengthways. With the aid of a teaspoon, scoop out the flesh which you will set aside in a bowl. Place the hollowed-out courgette shells in an oiled baking dish. Put the meat and the chopped onion, capers, olives and basil in the bowl containing the vegetable pulp. A few spoonfuls of tomato purée will bind the mixture better. Mix well, spoon the mixture into the "shells", drizzle a little olive oil over and place in a hot oven for about 30 minutes.

ZUCCHINE SOTT'OLIO
COURGETTES IN OIL

- 1 KG / 2 LBS COURGETTES (ZUCCHINI)
- 4 CLOVES OF GARLIC
- 3 ANCHOVY FILLETS
- A FEW MINT LEAVES
- OREGANO AND HOT RED PEPPER
- OLIVE OIL AND VINEGAR
- SALT

PREPARATION TIME: 30 MINUTES

CUT THE COURGETTES into "julienne" strips and blanch in a saucepan with two parts of salted water and one part of vinegar for 5 minutes.

Drain well and put into a jar or a bowl. Season with pieces of garlic, mint, oregano, hot red pepper, pieces of anchovy and a few drops of vinegar. Cover with olive oil. You may grill the courgettes instead of boiling them, if you like.

COURGETTES IN SICILY are mostly preserved in oil for keeping in the larder. This is an excellent "nibble" and may be used as a side-plate for meat or fish dishes or with hot bread.

PASTA, SOUP AND RICE DISHES

The recipes for pasta and rice dishes (served nowadays as a first course) have been collected all together for reasons of convenience because, in traditional popular Sicilian cuisine, such dishes formed the backbone of their one-course meals.

It would not be correct to speak of "pasta asciutta" (i.e., not in a broth or soup) because liquid sauces containing cooked and raw vegetables were always plentiful and were "soaked up" with bread which was never missing from the table. Only on Sundays and festive days was the sauce enhanced with meat balls, sausages or other meat.

Along coastal areas, the sauce was based on fish, generally tuna, bluefish or seafood (the poor man's meat).

Regarding the alimentation of common folk, dishes in the Sicilian kitchen were prepared according to certain rites. One such rite concerned the draining of pasta: it was to be lifted out of the saucepan with the aid of a long-handled wooden fork and placed on the serving dish. If the accompanying sauce required cheese, then this had to be sprinkled over the pasta before adding the sauce.

Pasta therefore is never really "asciutta" or dry because it is served with the most imaginative sauces, and the cooking water keeps it "gridda" or slithery. The pasta used to be made at home and varied in type depending on the sauce accompanying it.

The names of the dishes, even though adapted to the Sicilian tongue, are reminiscent of their countries of origin. "Tummala" or timbale, for example, seems to derive from the name of the Arab emir Thummel, who lived in Sicily for a long time. The "pasta alla Norma" is a classic dish from Catania in honour of the composer Bellini. Furthermore, in Catania's parlance, "norma" is an adjective qualifying something or someone that is "ne plus ultra". Included among the first course dishes are soups and those based on rice.

Almost no soups in Sicily are watery, certainly not those based on pulses and vegetables. Broth is a thing apart. The type of pasta to be added to the soups is chosen according to the kind of pulse employed. The pasta must be short, cylinder-shaped and ribbed and must be of the correct size to "hold" the pulses. Lentils are generally served with "Ave Marias", beans with "Pater Nosters", chick peas with "attuppateddi". When the broth becomes soup, the "u curadduzzu" are used, i.e. tiny pasta shapes the name of which recalls small, regularly-cut coral stars.

Vegetable soups are (or were) spring and summer dishes. Considered scarcely nutritious, soups were generally enhanced with pork rind, lard, pieces of cheese or marrow bone. Rice was held to be barely nutritious (today it has been revalued) and destined for consumption by the sick and convalescent. There is a proverb which goes:

> "Risu mi calu/E nun mi jisu"
> (Eating rice prostrates me
> and does not boost me up)

E. Alaimo "Proverbi siciliani" Edit. Martello

This consideration is held by the labourer hoeing away who warns that rice does not sufficiently sustain the strength of land workers. Rice dishes are not very numerous and are rather elaborate. The consumption of rice was concentrated around the feast day of Santa Lucia on 13 December. Indeed, the story goes that, in 1636, Sicily had been hit by appalling famine and the production of cereal was not sufficient to feed the population. Legend has it that, because of a violent (though providential) seastorm, a ship laden with rice and wheat was forced to anchor in the port of Syracuse on 12 December. In almost the whole of Sicily, neither bread nor pasta is eaten to honour Santa Lucia, but instead, both sweet and savoury dishes based on corn and rice are consumed - "cuccìa", rice patties, timbales, fritters and rice puddings, etc.

ARANCINE
RICE PATTIES

◆

- 1 KG / 2 LBS / 4 CUPS LONG-GRAIN RICE
- 800 G / 1¾ LBS MINCED (GROUND) MEAT
- 500 G / 1 LB PEAS
- 500 G / 1 LB / 5 CUPS DRIED BREADCRUMBS
- 300 G / ¾ LB FRESH CACIOCAVALLO OR SHARP PROVOLA CHEESE
- 100 G / 4 OZ / 1 CUP GRATED PECORINO OR PARMESAN CHEESE
- 1 MEDIUM ONION
- 7-8 EGGS
- 2 TBSP TOMATO PASTE OR 1 TIN (CAN) TOMATO CONCENTRATE
- 125 ML / 4 FL OZ / ½ CUP DRY WHITE WINE
- BASIL
- OIL FOR FRYING

◆

PREPARATION TIME: 4 HOURS

CHOP THE ONION and sauté in a little oil in a frying pan until golden. Add the meat and stir. Pour in the wine and allow to evaporate. Dilute the tomato concentrate in hot water and add to cover the meat completely.

Season with salt, pepper and basil. Simmer gently for about an hour. Add the peas and continue cooking for about 30 minutes. Stand a colander over a saucepan, pour in the sauce and separate out the solids from the liquid.

Cook the rice in plenty of salted water in a saucepan and drain while still firm (it still has to be fried). Return to the same pan, pour over some of the sauce and stir, adding more if necessary (the rice must be barely coloured).

Add the grated cheese and stir. When cold, add 2 whole eggs and stir. Meanwhile, close at hand, get ready a bowl with the breadcrumbs, a bowl with the diced cheese, a bowl in which to beat the remaining eggs, the saucepan with the rice and a bowl with water to dip your hands into.

Turn some dry breadcrumbs onto large platters which will hold the "arancine" once they are ready.

Take a small quantity of the cooked rice in your right hand and transfer it to your dampened left hand.

Make a shell which you will fill with a little of the meat and peas and 2/3 pieces of cheese.

Close up the patty with some more rice and, still with your hands, shape it into an "orange".

Egg-and-crumb it, compressing it in both hands, and place on the platter with the breadcrumbs. Continue until all the rice is used up. Deep fry in hot oil. To save on oil, I recommend using a not too large, deep-sided pan, frying 3 or 4 patties at a time.

CUSCUS ALLA TRAPANESE
COUSCOUS, TRAPANI-STYLE

♦

- 500 G / 1 LB / 3 CUPS PRE-COOKED COUSCOUS
- 1½ KG / 3 LBS MIXED FISH: E.G. DENTEX OR SEA BASS, GILTHEAD OR SEA BREAM, CUTTLEFISH, CLAMS, GROPER, RED MULLET, MUSSELS, SHELLFISH, ETC.
- 500 G / 1 LB RIPE TOMATOES
- 2 CLOVES OF GARLIC
- 2 STALKS OF CELERY
- 2 CARROTS
- 1 BAY LEAF
- 1 ONION
- 1 SPRIG OF PARSLEY
- 1 SACHET OF POWDERED SAFFRON
- PINCH PAPRIKA
- SALT AND PEPPER
- HOT RED PEPPER

♦

PREPARATION TIME: 4 HOURS

CUT, SCALE AND BONE THE FISH. Remove the shells from the crustaceans and the valves from the seafood. Put the fish trimmings into a saucepan with the shells, cover with water aromatised with half an onion, a few parsley stalks, a stick of celery and a carrot. Season with salt and pepper, boil for 30 minutes and filter the fish stock.

Sauté the remaining half of the onion in oil with a carrot, a stick of celery and some parsley, all chopped up, and the garlic clove left whole for removal as soon as it colours. First add the fish which require a longer cooking time, then the shellfish. Moisten with half of the filtered fish stock, add the tomato pulp and leave to cook for 15 minutes. Add the remaining fish, check the salt and continue cooking for 20 minutes, sprinkling with hot red pepper just before drawing off the heat. Pour the couscous into a large bowl and moisten with a cup of warm water in which you will have dissolved the paprika and saffron. Stir the semolina with your fingers, scooping it up to distribute the water uniformly. Pour the couscous into its special steamer or into a colander with holes on the bottom only, placed over a saucepan half full of water. Before putting on the hob (burner), seal the edges of the pan in contact with the colander with the aid of a cloth previously dampened and rubbed in flour. Wrap this around where the two saucepans meet so that it forms a kind of seal as it cools, which will prevent steam from escaping. Boil for about an hour, stirring the semolina from time to time (it must soak up the moisture, cooking in the steam). Pour the couscous into a roomy bowl, douse with the remaining fish stock and serve with the fish in its sauce.

THE WORD "COUSCOUS" is Arabic in origin and stands to mean little pieces. In fact, couscous consists of tiny lumps of semolina, obtained by working the semolina with rotary movements of the hand (dampened with water) in a special earthenware bowl called "mafaradda". The flour clings together forming tiny grains. The semolina can nowadays be bought already lumped together.

MINESTRA CON LE CASTAGNE
CHESTNUT SOUP

- 500 G / 1 LB DITALINI (SHORT PASTA TUBES)
- 1 KG / 2 LBS CHESTNUTS
- 2 BUNCHES WILD FENNEL LEAVES
- SALT AND PEPPER
- HOT RED PEPPER
- OLIVE OIL

PREPARATION TIME: 1 HOUR

MAKE A HALF-INCH slit on the chestnut skins and blanch them in boiling water for about 10 minutes. Peel and replace in the boiling water with the fennel cut into pieces. When the chestnuts are reduced to a pulp, add the ditalini, salt and hot red pepper and finish off cooking. If necessary, add more boiling water. You should end up with a creamy soup which is not watery. Serve with a trickle of uncooked olive oil.

THIS IS A TIME-HONOURED dish from the mountainous area of the Palermo district. A dear friend from Pollina passed on this recipe.

MINESTRA CON I CECI

CHICKPEA SOUP

- ■ 500 G / 1 LB DITALI (SHORT PASTA TUBES)
- ■ 500 G / 1 LB CHICKPEAS (GARBANZOS)
- ■ 2 SPRING ONIONS/SCALLIONS
- ■ PINCH OF BICARBONATE OF SODA (BAKING SODA)
- ■ A SPRIG OF ROSEMARY
- ■ SALT AND PEPPER
- ■ OLIVE OIL

PREPARATION TIME: 2½ HOURS

SOAK THE CHICKPEAS overnight in water with the bicarbonate of soda. Cook them gently in salted water for about 2 hours, together with the chopped onions and rosemary.

Season with olive oil and pepper and add the pasta previously boiled in salted water. This may be eaten with chunks of stale bread, barely moistened and then fried in hot oil.

PREPARED IN AN EARTHENWARE POT, this is a traditional first course for St Joseph's feast day. It is often enhanced with other pulses (legumes), cooked very simply in boiling water with onion, salt and pepper. As the various pulses have different cooking times, they are only mixed together once cooked and then seasoned with olive oil.

MINESTRA CON IL FORMAGGIO
CHEESE AND TOMATO SOUP

◆

- 500 G / 1 LB / 2½ CUPS HOME-MADE TOMATO SAUCE
- 500 G / 1 LB SOFT CACIOCAVALLO OR A TUSCAN OR SARDINIAN CACIOTTA CHEESE
- 4 SLICES BREAD, TOASTED OR FRIED
- 1 LARGE ONION
- PARSLEY
- SALT
- PEPPER OR HOT RED PEPPER
- OLIVE OIL

◆

PREPARATION TIME: 30 MINUTES

GENTLY FRY THE CHOPPED ONION and parsley in a little oil in a saucepan, adding the tomato sauce, salt, pepper (or hot red pepper) and the caciocavallo cut to pieces. Cook the cheese soup slowly for 15 minutes. Serve with slices of toasted or fried bread.

THIS IS A "BAGNA PANI" SOUP for dipping bread into. Cheese substitutes the traditional fish and the cooking method is the same as for fish soup.

MINESTRA CON I FAGIOLI
BEAN AND PASTA SOUP

- **500 G / 1 LB DITALI** (SHORT PASTA TUBES)
- **500 G / 1 LB RED KIDNEY** OR PINTO BEANS
- **200 G / 8 OZ PORK RIND**
- **1 ONION**
- **PINCH OF BICARBONATE OF SODA (BAKING SODA)**
- **PEPPER OR HOT RED PEPPER**

PREPARATION TIME: 1 HOUR

SOAK THE BEANS OVERNIGHT in water with a pinch of bicarbonate of soda. Sauté the finely-sliced or chopped onion in a little oil, together with the pork rind. Add the beans, drained of the water containing the soda, and cover with hot water. Season with salt and pepper and leave to simmer gently for about 45 minutes. Add hot water and check the salt. When the water boils, pour in the pasta and cook. Dress with uncooked olive oil and hot red pepper.

VARIATION: to give the dish more flavour, add a marrow bone and a tablespoon of home-made tomato sauce during cooking.

MINESTRA CON LE LENTICCHIE
VEGETABLE SOUP WITH LENTILS

- **500 G / 1 LB CONTINENTAL LENTILS**
- **400 G / 14 OZ DITALINI** OR BROKEN UP SPAGHETTI
- **3 DRIED TOMATOES**
- **1 ONION**
- **A FEW CELERY LEAVES**
- **SALT**
- **PEPPER OR HOT RED PEPPER**
- **OLIVE OIL**

PREPARATION TIME: 1½ HOURS

PLACE THE LENTILS in water seasoned with salt and pepper in a pan, adding the chopped onion and the dried tomatoes and celery leaves cut to pieces. Leave to cook for about 1 hour. Boil the pasta separately, or else top up the lentils with hot water, check the salt and throw in the pasta when the water starts to boil. Season with olive oil, pepper or hot red pepper.

MINESTRA CON I TENERUMI

PASTA WITH COURGETTE (ZUCCHINI) LEAVES

- 500 G / 1 LB BROKEN UP SPAGHETTI
- 150 G / 6 OZ DICED CACIOCAVALLO OR SHARP PROVALA CHEESE
- 2 BUNCHES OF THE TENDER STALKS AND LEAVES OF COURGETTE (ZUCCHINI) PLANTS OR SWISS CHARD
- 2 RIPE TOMATOES
- 2 CLOVES OF GARLIC
- SALT
- PEPPER
- OLIVE OIL

PREPARATION TIME: 30 MINUTES

CUT THE LEAVES and the tender parts of the stalks up into small pieces, rinse and cook in boiling salted water. After 10-15 minutes, throw in the spaghetti. Gently fry the whole garlic cloves in a little oil in a small saucepan (removing them as soon as they colour) and the tomatoes, skinned and cut into pieces, stripped of their seeds. Cook for about 10 minutes and then pour into the saucepan with the "tenerumi" and the pasta. Before drawing off the heat, add the diced cheese.

MINESTRA D'ORZO

BARLEY SOUP

- 2L / 4 PTS / 8 CUPS CHICKEN STOCK
- 500 G / 1 LB BARLEY FLOUR OR PEARL BARLEY
- 250 G / 8 OZ FRESH PECORINO OR ANOTHER FULL-FLAVOURED CHEESE
- 2 RIPE TOMATOES
- A FEW MINT LEAVES (OPTIONAL)
- SALT
- PEPPER

PREPARATION TIME: 1½ HOURS

COOK THE BOILING FOWL in salted water. Remove when cooked.

Add the tomatoes, skinned, seeded and cut into pieces, to the broth.

When the broth comes back to the boil, sprinkle the barley flour over, stirring well to prevent lumps from forming. Cook for 15 minutes over a low flame, add the mint and the diced cheese and draw off the heat. Serve hot. This is a delicate soup which is excellent for children, the elderly and those convalescing.

MINESTRA DI FAVE SECCHE

DRY BROAD BEAN SOUP

- 500 G / 1 LB SHELLED DRY BROAD BEANS
- 2 BUNCHES SWISS CHARD OR SPINACH (ABOUT 400 G /14 OZ)
- 1 MEDIUM-SIZED ONION

◆

PREPARATION TIME: 2 HOURS

SOAK THE DRY BROAD BEANS OVERNIGHT. Cook for an hour in salted water over gentle heat. Drain and mash with a fork. Wash the chard and boil in salted water. While they are cooking, gently sauté the chopped onion in a saucepan, then add the broad beans and the greens, cut up. Season with salt, pepper and uncooked olive oil.

VARIATION: you can add short pasta or broken spaghetti to enrich this dish.

MINESTRA DI FAVE VERDI
FRESH BROAD BEAN SOUP

- 1 KG / 2 LBS BROAD BEANS IN PODS OR 500 G /1 LB SHELLED
- 400 G / 14 OZ DITALINI OR BROKEN UP SPAGHETTI
- 50 G / 2 OZ / 8 TBSP GRATED PECORINO OR PARMESAN CHEESE (OPTIONAL)
- 2 SPRING ONIONS/ SCALLIONS
- BUNCH OF FENNEL (OPTIONAL)
- HOT RED PEPPER

PREPARATION TIME: 1 HOUR

BROWN THE CHOPPED ONIONS in a deep-sided saucepan. Add the shelled broad beans and the washed fennel leaves cut into pieces. Season with salt and pepper. Cover with hot water and leave to cook, stirring frequently and breaking up the beans. When the beans are cooked, top up with about a litre (2 pints/4 cups) of hot water, check the salt, and when it comes back to the boil, throw in the pasta. Cook until the pasta is ready.

THE BROAD BEANS used here are still green, but no longer very tender. This dish is a modern version of a more ancient one where dry beans were used.

The women used to prepare plenty of "maccu" in the evening so that enough was left over for the menfolk to take for lunch in the fields the following day.

MINESTRA DI FRUMENTO (FARRO)
EMMER SOUP

- 4 BUNCHES OF FENNEL OR SWISS CHARD
- 400 G / 14 OZ / 2½ CUPS EMMER (WHEAT BERRY)
- 50 G / 2 OZ / 6 TBSP GRATED PECORINO OR PARMESAN CHEESE
- SALT
- PEPPER OR HOT RED PEPPER
- OLIVE OIL

PREPARATION TIME: 1 HOUR

WASH THE FENNEL LEAVES (or the Swiss chard) and boil in salted water. When cooked, add a little water and, as soon as it comes back to the boil, sprinkle in the emmer, stirring constantly. Cook slowly for 20 minutes until the soup is nice and thick.
Season with olive oil, grated cheese and pepper or hot red pepper.

VARIATION: this dish may be eaten cold or else it can be put into an oiled baking tin (pan), cut into rectangles, seasoned with roughly-chopped, skinned tomatoes (fresh or tinned), pitted black olives, a few anchovy fillets and olive oil and then cooked in a hot oven for 10 minutes.

MINESTRA DI PATATE
POTATO SOUP

- 500 G / 1 LB DITALINI OR BROKEN UP SPAGHETTI
- 50 G / 2 OZ / 8 TBSP GRATED PECORINO OR PARMESAN CHEESE
- 4-5 LARGE POTATOES
- 2-3 RIPE TOMATOES
- 1 MEDIUM-SIZED ONION
- BASIL
- SALT AND PEPPER

PREPARATION TIME: 30 MINUTES

SAUTÉ THE CHOPPED onion in a little oil, add the potatoes (peeled, washed and diced) and break up the skinned, seeded tomatoes. Season with basil, salt and pepper, cover the potatoes with a cup of hot water and leave to cook for 20-30 minutes. Boil the pasta, drain while still "al dente", dredge with grated cheese and add the potatoes.

MINESTRA DI PATATE, ZUCCHINE E MELANZANE
POTATO, COURGETTE AND AUBERGINE SOUP

- 400 G / 14 OZ DITALINI OR BROKEN UP SPAGHETTI
- 50 G / 2 OZ / 8 TBSP GRATED PECORINO OR PARMESAN CHEESE
- 2 POTATOES
- 2 FRESH TOMATOES
- 1 MEDIUM-SIZED COURGETTE (ZUCCHINI) OR 2-3 SMALL ONES
- 1 AUBERGINE OR EGGPLANT
- A FEW BASIL LEAVES
- OLIVE OIL

PREPARATION TIME: 1 HOUR

CUT UP THE aubergines, potatoes and courgette(s) into chunks. Sauté the chopped onion in a saucepan with a little oil and add the vegetables cut into chunks. Mix well. Throw in the skinned and roughly-chopped tomatoes. Aromatise with basil, season with salt and pepper and add a glass of hot water to cover the vegetables. Cook for about 20 minutes. Check the salt and top up with water (which must always be hot). Throw in the pasta when it boils. Cook until just firm.

MINESTRA SAPORITA DI PANE
BREAD SOUP

- 200 G / 8 OZ / ½ LB STALE BREAD
- 1 CLOVE OF GARLIC
- 2 RIPE TOMATOES
- BASIL
- SALT
- PEPPER
- OLIVE OIL

PREPARATION TIME: 1 HOUR

SAUTÉ THE GARLIC, either chopped or whole, add the stale bread, cover with water and add the skinned tomatoes, stripped of seeds and roughly chopped. Season with salt and a few torn-up basil leaves and leave to cook for 10 minutes. Sprinkle over a little oil and pepper.

VARIATION: if you like, you may try adding some cheese cut into dice, or meat left-overs, and use broth instead of water.

MINESTRONE
VEGETABLE SOUP

- 500 G / 1 LB POTATOES
- 500 G / 1 LB FRESH WHITE HARICOT BEANS
- 500 G / 1 LB VEGETABLES IN SEASON
- 1L / 2 PTS / 4 CUPS MEAT STOCK (OR FROM A BOUILLON CUBE)
- 2-3 TOMATOES
- 1 ONION
- 1 STICK OF CELERY
- SALT AND PEPPER
- OLIVE OIL

PREPARATION TIME: 1½ HOURS

CLEAN THE VEGETABLES and cut into pieces. Brown the chopped onion in a little oil and add the skinned, seeded and roughly-chopped tomatoes.
Cook for a few minutes, add the vegetables and season with salt and pepper.
Pour in the stock and leave to cook for about an hour over a low flame. If you wish, short noodles or rice or pieces of toasted bread may be added.

MINESTRONE is a seasonal dish. Only fresh vegetables of the season are used and the quantities always tend to differ.
It may be enriched with crusts of cheese, meat, pasta or cubes of toast soaked in milk and fried. You may serve it as cream of vegetable soup, putting the vegetables through a food mill, or with the vegetables cut into more or less regular pieces.

ANELLETTI AL FORNO
BAKED PASTA

- ◆ -

- **500 G / 1 LB ANELLETTI OR PENNE (UNRIBBED SHORT PASTA)**
- **500 G / 1 LB MINCED (GROUND) MEAT**
- **400 G / 14 OZ / 2 CUPS SHELLED PEAS**
- **100 G / 4 OZ / 1 CUP GRATED PECORINO OR PARMESAN CHEESE**
- **300 G / ¾ LB PRIMOSALE OR FRESH CHEESE**
- **1 TBSP TOMATO EXTRACT OR A TIN (CAN) TOMATO CONCENTRATE**
- **1 MEDIUM-SIZED ONION**
- **125 ML / 8 TBSP DRY WHITE WINE**
- **BASIL**
- **SALT AND PEPPER**

- ◆ -

PREPARATION TIME: 3 HOURS

SAUTÉ THE CHOPPED ONION in a little oil in a large saucepan and add the minced meat. Stir and pour in the wine after a few minutes, allowing to evaporate. Then add the tomato extract dissolved in hot water or the tomato concentrate. After half-an-hour over the flame, add the peas and leave to cook a further 20 minutes. Filter and set the liquid aside. Cook the pasta in boiling salted water and drain while still quite "al dente". Pour the pasta back into its saucepan and pour in a little of the sauce and the grated cheese. Oil a baking tin or dish, sprinkle dry breadcrumbs over and make a layer of pasta on the bottom. Cover with some of the meat sauce and slices of primosale cheese. Continue layering the ingredients until they have all been used up. Bake in a hot oven for about 20 minutes.

THE OLD RECIPE used a "ragù" which was not made up using raw minced meat but cooked chunks of meat (beef and pork) which were then chopped up with the aid of a "mezzaluna" knife.

PASTA AL NERO DI SEPPIA
BLACK INKFISH PASTA

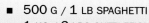

- 500 G / 1 LB SPAGHETTI
- 1 KG / 2 LBS CUTTLEFISH
- 100 G / 4 OZ / 2 CUPS GRATED PECORINO CHEESE
- 1 TSP TOMATO CONCENTRATE
- 1 MEDIUM-SIZED, WHITE-SKINNED ONION
- PARSLEY
- SALT AND PEPPER
- OLIVE OIL

PREPARATION TIME: 45 MINUTES

SKIN, GUT AND BONE THE CUTTLEFISH and, putting the ink sac aside, cut into strips. Sauté the chopped onion in a little oil in a saucepan, add the cuttlefish, the tomato concentrate dissolved in half-a-glass of hot water and the black ink of the mollusc. Cook until the sauce has reduced and season with salt and pepper.

Boil the spaghetti, drain while still firm to the tooth and serve with the sauce.

THIS DISH was originally from the eastern side of Sicily and it is also found in Venetian cookery. The sauce is particularly tasty, though those who are not familiar with it must overcome their impact with the murky aspect of the black sauce with pearly reflections.

PASTA AL NERO DI SEPPIA E PISELLI
BLACK INKFISH PASTA WITH PEAS

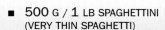

- 500 G / 1 LB SPAGHETTINI (VERY THIN SPAGHETTI)
- 1 KG / 2 LBS CUTTLEFISH
- 500 G / 1 LB / 2 CUPS SHELLED PEAS
- 500 G / 1 LB RIPE TOMATOES
- 1 MEDIUM-SIZED, WHITE-SKINNED ONION
- 125 ML / ½ CUP DRY WHITE WINE
- PARSLEY
- SALT
- HOT RED PEPPER

PREPARATION TIME: 45 MINUTES

SKIN, GUT AND BONE THE CUTTLEFISH, putting aside the ink sac, and cut into strips. Pour a little oil into a (preferably) earthenware pot and sauté the chopped onion. Add the cuttlefish strips and sprinkle the white wine over.

Once evaporated, add the skinned, seeded and roughly-chopped tomatoes, the peas and the black ink from the sacs. Cook until the sauce has reduced and season with salt and pepper. Before drawing off the heat, add the chopped parsley. Boil the spaghetti, drain while still "al dente" and pour the sauce over.

IN THE PALERMO DISTRICT, black inkfish pasta served complete with their ink has the variation of the addition of peas.

Peas in Sicily, and particularly around Palermo, are generally added to sauces. They are rarely eaten as a vegetable dish.

PASTA ALLA CARRETTIERA
PASTA WITH A PIQUANT SAUCE

- **500 G / 1 LB BUCATINI** (PASTA STRAWS)
- **1 KG / 2 LBS RIPE TOMATOES**
- **200 G / 8 OZ / 2 CUPS GRATED PECORINO CHEESE OR SALTED RICOTTA**
- **5-6 BASIL LEAVES**
- **2 CLOVES OF GARLIC**
- **SALT**
- **HOT RED PEPPER**
- **OLIVE OIL**

PREPARATION TIME: 30 MINUTES

PUT THE CHOPPED GARLIC, basil and hot red pepper into a bowl. Peel the tomatoes and cut to pieces, mix well with the chopped garlic, basil and hot red pepper. Add a little oil and leave to steep.

Boil the bucatini in plenty of salted water, drain while still firm to the tooth and pour into the bowl of tomatoes. Dredge with the salted ricotta or grated cheese and stir.

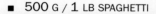

VARIATION: you may substitute parsley for basil and add 4 cut-up anchovy fillets, omitting the tomato in this case.

PASTA ALLA CONTADINA
SPAGHETTI WITH TOMATO AND ANCHOVY SAUCE

- **500 G / 1 LB SPAGHETTI**
- **500 G / 1 LB RIPE TOMATOES OR A TIN (CAN) SKINNED TOMATOES (2½ CUPS)**
- **4 ANCHOVY FILLETS**
- **1-2 CLOVES OF GARLIC**
- **BASIL**
- **OREGANO**
- **SALT AND PEPPER**
- **OLIVE OIL**

PREPARATION TIME: 20 MINUTES

DISSOLVE THE ANCHOVIES in the oil in a saucepan which is preferably in earthenware. Add the chopped garlic, the tomatoes, stripped of their seeds and cut to pieces, the basil and the oregano. Cook for a few minutes and pour over the spaghetti as soon as it is cooked and drained "al dente".

This dish has a lovely aroma and is very quick to prepare if you get the sauce ready while the spaghetti is cooking.

PASTA ALLA NORMA
SPAGHETTI WITH AUBERGINE AND TOMATO SAUCE

◆

- 500 G / 1 LB SPAGHETTI
- 1 KG / 2 LBS RIPE TOMATOES
- 200 G / 8 OZ / 2 GENEROUS CUPS GRATED SALTED RICOTTA CHEESE
- 3 AUBERGINES (EGGPLANTS)
- 3 CLOVES OF GARLIC
- 2 MEDIUM-SIZED ONIONS
- PLENTY OF BASIL
- OLIVE OIL
- SALT
- PEPPER

◆

PREPARATION TIME: 1 HOUR

SLICE THE AUBERGINES and put them in a bowl with salted water for about an hour. Prepare the tomato sauce in the meantime: put the roughly-chopped tomatoes and onion, the whole garlic and the basil in a saucepan. Season with salt and simmer gently until all the liquid has evaporated. Rub the sauce through a sieve or food mill and dress with uncooked olive oil. Remove the aubergines from their soaking water, squeeze and dry them and fry in some hot oil in a frying pan. Boil the spaghetti in plenty of salted water. As soon as cooked to the "al dente" stage, remove from the pan with a long-handled fork, drain and arrange on a serving platter.

Sprinkle half the grated ricotta over and cover with the tomato sauce.

Stir well, garnish with fresh basil leaves and with four aubergine slices.

Serve at table. Each diner will add, to his taste, some more salted ricotta, pepper and fried aubergine.

PASTA CON I BROCCOLI AL FORNO
BAKED CAULIFLOWER CHEESE WITH RIGATONI

♦

- 500 G / 1 LB RIGATONI (SHORT, FLUTED PASTA)
- 1 KG / 2 LBS CAULIFLOWER*
- 500 G / 1 LB SAUSAGES
- 300 G / ¾ LB / 1½ CUPS TOMATO PULP
- 300 G / ¾ LB FRESH CACIOCAVALLO CHEESE
- 100 G / 4 OZ / 1 CUP GRATED PECORINO CHEESE
- 300 G / ¾ LB MINCED (GROUND) MEAT
- 2 MEDIUM-SIZED ONIONS
- 125 ML / 8 TBSP DRY WHITE WINE
- SALT
- PEPPER
- OLIVE OIL

♦

PREPARATION TIME: 1 HOUR

BOIL THE CAULIFLOWER, drain and conserve the cooking water. Chop one onion finely, brown gently in a pan and add the cauliflower in small florets.

In another pan, gently fry the other chopped onion in a little oil, add the minced meat and the skinned and crumbled sausages.

Add the wine and cook for a few minutes to allow it to evaporate.

Pour in the tomato pulp and a glass of water. Simmer over low heat until the sauce is semi-liquid.

Toss the cauliflower into the sauce and stir well.

Divide the sauce into three equal parts.

One part will be mixed with the rigatoni, which will be boiled in the cauliflower cooking water.

Another part will cover half the pasta which has been poured into an oiled baking dish and then sprinkled with grated cheese.

Make another layer of rigatoni, cover with the remaining sauce and dust with grated cheese.

Slice the caciocavallo and arrange on top of the pasta. Bake in a hot oven for about half-an-hour.

THIS PASTA is called "ncasciata" or "embedded" because set in a quite shallow, rectangular baking dish. This dish is also served up at wedding feasts because it is considered to bring good luck.

The pasta chosen is short and ribbed because it traps the sauce better than plain, smooth macaroni.
* Sicilians use the term broccoli to mean cauliflower.

PASTA CON I CARCIOFI

PASTA WITH ARTICHOKES

- 500 G / 1 LB SPAGHETTI
- 200 G / 8 OZ FRESH PECORINO OR ANOTHER TYPE OF FRESH CHEESE
- 100 G / 4 OZ / 1 CUP GRATED PECORINO OR PARMESAN CHEESE
- 5 TENDER GLOBE ARTICHOKES
- 2 CLOVES OF GARLIC
- 125 ML / 8 TBSP WHITE WINE
- PARSLEY

PREPARATION TIME: 45 MINUTES

CLEAN THE ARTICHOKES, removing the tough outer leaves. Cut across into strips and soak in water into which you have squeezed half a lemon. Sauté the garlic in a little oil in a casserole, add the artichokes, stir and pour on the white wine.

When it has evaporated, add a glass of hot water and cook the vegetables for about 10 minutes. Add the chopped parsley before drawing off the heat.

Cook the spaghetti until "al dente" and drain. Return to the same pan and sprinkle the grated cheese over with half the artichokes.

Oil a baking dish and pour in half the spaghetti. Dredge with pieces of fresh cheese and the remaining artichokes. Cover with the rest of the spaghetti, sprinkle with grated cheese and bake in a hot oven for 15 minutes.

PASTA CON IL CAVOLFIORE
CAULIFLOWER WITH PASTA AND CHEESE SAUCE

◆

- 500 G / 1 LB BUCATINI (PASTA STRAWS)
- 1 KG / 2 LBS CAULIFLOWER
- 100 G / 4 OZ / 1 CUP GRATED CACIOCAVALLO, PECORINO OR PARMESAN CHEESE
- 25 G / 1 OZ / 4 TBSP PINE-NUTS
- 50 G / 2 OZ / ⅓ CUP RAISINS
- 4-5 ANCHOVY FILLETS
- ¼ TSP SAFFRON
- 1 LARGE ONION
- SALT AND PEPPER
- OLIVE OIL

◆

PREPARATION TIME: 45 MINUTES

DISCARD THE CENTRAL CORE of the cauliflower and boil the vegetable in salted water. Drain while still firm, reserving the cooking water. Put the anchovies, olive oil and chopped onion in a large frying pan and sauté gently, crushing the anchovies with a wooden spoon. Add the raisins, pine-nuts and the boiled cauliflower florets. Cook for about 10 minutes, mashing the cauliflower to blend in the flavours. In the cauliflower cooking water, boil the pasta until "al dente". Just before turning off the heat, dissolve the saffron in the water. Remove the pasta from the saucepan with the aid of a long-handled fork and place in the saucepan with the cauliflower. Dress with the grated cheese. Mix well and serve.

VARIATION: mix the pasta with half of the cauliflower and arrange in an oiled baking dish. Add the rest of the sauce, sprinkle all the grated cheese on top and trickle a stream of olive oil over. Bake in a hot oven for 15 minutes until a golden crust has formed.

PASTA CON IL CAVOLFIORE E LA RICOTTA

PASTA WITH CAULIFLOWER AND RICOTTA

- 500 G / 1 LB DITALI OR BUCATINI (SHORT PASTA TUBES)
- 1 KG / 2 LBS CAULIFLOWER
- 500 G / 1 LB / 2¾ CUPS RICOTTA CHEESE
- 2 EGGS
- 100 G / 4 OZ / 1 CUP GRATED PECORINO OR PARMESAN CHEESE
- SALT, PEPPER, OIL

PREPARATION TIME: 45 MINUTES

BOIL THE CAULIFLOWER AND DRAIN, keeping the cooking water. Gently fry the cauliflower in a little oil in a frying pan. Reserve a little of the cauliflower cooking water to soften the ricotta in, mashing it with the aid of a fork. Boil the pasta in the rest of the water, check the salt, drain while still firm and pour into the bowl with the ricotta. Stir well and add a little freshly-ground pepper.

Oil a baking dish and arrange alternate layers of pasta and of cauliflower until the ingredients are used up (you may get two or three layers). Beat the eggs with the grated cheese and pour over the top layer. Bake in a hot oven until a golden crust forms.

PASTA CON IL PANGRATTATO
PASTA WITH BREADCRUMB SAUCE

◆

- 500 G / 1 LB BUCATINI (PASTA STRAWS)
- 500 G / 1 LB WILD FENNEL LEAVES (OPTIONAL)
- 150 G / 6 OZ / 1½ CUPS DRY BREADCRUMBS
- 5 ANCHOVY FILLETS
- 30 G / 1 OZ / 3 TBSP SULTANAS OR RAISINS
- 30 G / 1 OZ / 4 TBSP PINE-NUTS
- 1 CLOVE OF GARLIC
- PARSLEY

◆

PREPARATION TIME: 30 MINUTES

CLEAN THE FENNEL LEAVES and boil in salted water. Drain (keeping the cooking water for boiling the pasta in) and chop.

In a small saucepan, place the anchovy fillets and the garlic, chopped or else left whole, for easy removal once browned. Press down on the anchovies with a fork until they dissolve. Add the fennel leaves, sultanas and pine-nuts. Brown the breadcrumbs in a very little oil in a frying pan, stirring continuously. Add the fennel leaves, together with the sultanas, pine-nuts and breadcrumbs. Stir.

Meanwhile, cook the bucatini which you will drain while "al dente". Turn into the serving bowl, toss in the breadcrumb mixture and the chopped parsley. Mix well and serve.

PASTA CON I PEPERONI
PASTA WITH SWEET PEPPER SAUCE

◆

- 500 G / 1 LB RIGATONI OR PENNE (SHORT NOODLES)
- 500 G / 1 LB / RIPE TOMATOES
- SWEET (BELL) PEPPERS
- 3 ANCHOVY FILLETS
- 1 CLOVE OF GARLIC
- 1 SPRIG OF PARSLEY
- 100 G / 4 OZ / 1 CUP GRATED PECORINO (OR OTHER SAVOURY CHEESE)
- HOT RED PEPPER
- SALT
- OLIVE OIL

◆

PREPARATION TIME: 1 HOUR

BAKE THREE OF THE PEPPERS IN THE OVEN. Skin and cut into small pieces.

Sauté the whole clove of garlic (which you will then remove) in oil in a frying pan. Add the roughly-chopped, skinned tomatoes, a raw pepper cut very thinly and a chopped-up anchovy. Cook for 10-15 minutes, add the hot red pepper and the chopped parsley and turn off the heat.

Boil the pasta in plenty of salted water, drain while still firm and dust with the grated pecorino cheese. Pour the sauce over and serve.

VARIATION: fry the cleaned, roughly-chopped peppers, then add a chopped-up mixture of one garlic clove, 30 g (1 oz / 2 tbsp) capers and 50 g (2 oz / ⅓ cup) stoned green olives. Allow the flavours to mingle. Add five ripe tomatoes, cut into pieces, and cook for 10 minutes. Before turning off the heat, sprinkle with a little chopped parsley.

Pour over the spaghetti and serve.

PASTA CON IL PESTO ALLA TRAPANESE

TRAPANI PASTA WITH "PESTO"

- 500 G / 1 LB SPAGHETTI
- 500 G / 1 LB RIPE TOMATOES
- 1 OR 2 CLOVES OF GARLIC
- 10 BASIL LEAVES
- 100 G / 4 OZ / 1 CUP GRATED PECORINO CHEESE
- 30 G / 1 OZ / ¼ CUP FRESH OR DRY, CHOPPED, SKINNED ALMONDS
- SALT AND PEPPER
- OLIVE OIL

PREPARATION TIME: 30 MINUTES

POUND THE GARLIC in a mortar together with the basil, almonds and a little olive oil (nowadays an electric blender can be used).

Transfer to a bowl and stir, adding a little olive oil and the grated pecorino.

Skin the tomatoes, discard their seeds, chop roughly and add the garlic and basil. Mix well and leave to rest.

Meanwhile, cook the spaghetti in plenty of salted water, drain while "al dente" and turn into the sauce bowl. Mix well and serve.

THIS USED to be a summer dish to eat while the almonds were still very tender.

91

PASTA CON IL POMODORO
SPAGHETTI WITH TOMATO SAUCE

- 500 G / 1 LB SPAGHETTI
- 1 KG / 2 LBS RIPE TOMATOES
- 500 G / 1 LB ONIONS
- 100 G / 4 OZ / 1 CUP GRATED PECORINO OR SALTED RICOTTA CHEESE
- 3 CLOVES OF GARLIC
- BASIL
- SALT AND PEPPER
- HOT RED PEPPER
- OLIVE OIL

PREPARATION TIME: 45 MINUTES

PUT THE ROUGHLY-CHOPPED tomatoes, the quartered onions, the cloves of garlic, the washed basil (without the stalks), salt and pepper into a saucepan. Simmer gently until all the liquid has evaporated. Sieve the sauce and season with olive oil. Boil the spaghetti in plenty of salted water, drain while "al dente", turn into a bowl and pour the sauce over. Separately, serve basil leaves, the grated pecorino or salted ricotta and the hot red pepper. Any type of pasta can be served with this sauce.

PASTA CON IL POMODORO PELATO
SPAGHETTI WITH "PICCHI PACCHIU" TOMATO SAUCE

- 500 G / 1 LB SPAGHETTI
- 500 G/ 1 LB RIPE TOMATOES
- 150 G / 6 OZ / 1½ CUPS GRATED PECORINO OR PARMESAN CHEESE
- 2 CLOVES OF GARLIC
- SALT
- PEPPER OR HOT RED PEPPER
- OLIVE OIL

PREPARATION TIME: 30 MINUTES

USE A SAUCEPAN, preferably in earthenware, for sautéing the chopped cloves of garlic in a little oil. Add the roughly-chopped, skinned tomatoes. Season with salt and pepper.
Simmer gently, crushing the tomatoes and stirring them with a wooden spoon until all the liquid has evaporated.
Boil the pasta in plenty of salted water, remove from the saucepan with the aid of a long-handled fork and plunge into the sauce in the pan.
Stir well. Serve the grated cheese separately.

THE ETYMON of the expression "picchi pacchiu" can be attributed to the splashing sound that the wooden spoon makes when it thuds against the tomato pieces to break them up.

PASTA CON IL POMODORO CRUDO PICCANTE
SPAGHETTI WITH UNCOOKED, PIQUANT TOMATO SAUCE

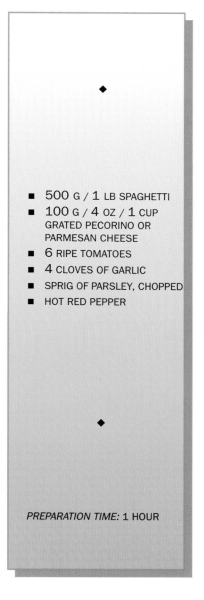

- 500 G / 1 LB SPAGHETTI
- 100 G / 4 OZ / 1 CUP GRATED PECORINO OR PARMESAN CHEESE
- 6 RIPE TOMATOES
- 4 CLOVES OF GARLIC
- SPRIG OF PARSLEY, CHOPPED
- HOT RED PEPPER

PREPARATION TIME: 1 HOUR

CUT UP THE SKINNED and seeded tomatoes in a bowl and add the garlic, pounded or chopped up with the parsley. Season with salt, hot red pepper and olive oil. Leave to steep for about 45 minutes. Boil the spaghetti in salted water, drain while "al dente" and arrange over the sauce.
Stir and serve with grated cheese apart.

PASTA CON IL POLPO
PASTA WITH OCTOPUS

◆

- 500 G / 1 LB RIBBED DITALI (SHORT PASTA TUBES)
- 1 KG / 2 LBS OCTOPUS
- 1 KG / 2 LBS RIPE TOMATOES
- 1 MEDIUM-SIZED ONION
- 125 ML / 8 TBSP DRY WHITE WINE
- SALT AND PEPPER
- PARSLEY

◆

PREPARATION TIME: 1 HOUR

CUT THE OCTOPUS into pieces, wash and cook in a casserole with salted water.

When all the water has been absorbed, add the chopped onion and the oil.

Fry gently, pour in the white wine and the skinned tomatoes, seeded and roughly-chopped. Season with salt and pepper and add plenty of hot water before throwing in the pasta.

When cooked, serve with the addition of chopped parsley.

THIS IS A FISHERMAN'S dish from the Palermo area. It is served as a first course and as a single-course meal.

PASTA CON L'AGGLASSATO
PASTA AND BRAISED BEEF

◆

- 500 G / 1 LB BUCATINI (PASTA STRAWS)
- 1 KG / 2 LBS TOPSIDE OF BEEF (BEEF ROAST)
- 1 KG / 2 LBS WHITE-SKINNED ONIONS
- 100 G / 4 OZ / 1 CUP GRATED PECORINO OR PARMESAN CHEESE
- ¼ L / ½ PT / 1¼ CUPS DRY WHITE WINE
- 2 TBSP HOME-MADE TOMATO SAUCE
- 1-2 SAGE LEAVES
- 1 BAY LEAF
- 1 SPRIG OF ROSEMARY
- 125 ML / ½ CUP OLIVE OIL
- FRESHLY-GROUND BLACK PEPPER

◆

PREPARATION TIME: 2½ HOURS

CHOP THE ONIONS and sweat in the oil without frying them. Sear the meat with the herbs in a saucepan and cover with the onions. Add the white wine and cook over gentle heat for about an hour, not forgetting to turn the meat over from time to time. When cooked, carve it into thin slices for serving as the main course. Put the onion through the food mill and add the tomato purée. Pour a third of the sauce over the meat.

Boil the bucatini in plenty of salted water. When cooked "al dente", remove with the aid of a long-handled fork and place on a serving dish. Pour the remaining sauce over and serve for the first course. Everybody will help himself to grated cheese and pepper.

PASTA CON LA BOTTARGA
PASTA WITH TUNA ROES

- 500 G / 1 LB BUCATINI (PASTA STRAWS)
- 150 G / 6 OZ / ⅔ CUP TUNA ROES
- 2-3 CLOVES OF GARLIC
- PLENTY OF CHOPPED PARSLEY
- HOT RED PEPPER (OPTIONAL)
- OLIVE OIL

PREPARATION TIME: 30 MINUTES

POUR A LITTLE OIL into a saucepan and gently sauté the chopped garlic and the roes, cut into pieces.

Stir and crush the roes with a fork to blend them in.

Remove from the heat and add the chopped parsley. Boil the bucatini in plenty of lightly-salted water. With the aid of a long-handled fork, turn it into a bowl and add the sauce. Mix well and serve.

Pass some botargo (tuna roe relish) round the table for grating over each plate.

PASTA CON LA RICOTTA

PASTA WITH RICOTTA CHEESE

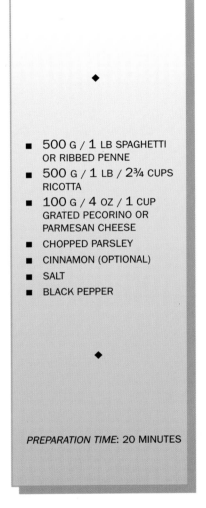

◆

- 500 G / 1 LB SPAGHETTI OR RIBBED PENNE
- 500 G / 1 LB / 2¾ CUPS RICOTTA
- 100 G / 4 OZ / 1 CUP GRATED PECORINO OR PARMESAN CHEESE
- CHOPPED PARSLEY
- CINNAMON (OPTIONAL)
- SALT
- BLACK PEPPER

◆

PREPARATION TIME: 20 MINUTES

PUT THE RICOTTA IN A BOWL, season with salt, pepper and cinnamon, and crush well with a fork. Boil the pasta in plenty of salted water, drain while still firm and add to the ricotta in the bowl. Pour in a little of the water that the pasta was cooked in and stir. Sprinkle with parsley and serve the cheese separately at table.

THIS USED TO BE A SPRING DISH. At this time of the year, the grass for grazing is very tender, so the ricotta is particularly mild.

PASTA CON LE SARDE
PASTA WITH SARDINES

♦
- 1 KG / 2 LBS BUCATINI (PASTA STRAWS)
- 1 KG / 2 LBS FRESH SARDINES
- 500 G / 1 LB WILD MOUNTAIN FENNEL LEAVES
- 5-6 ANCHOVY FILLETS
- 50 G / 2 OZ / ⅔ CUP CHOPPED TOASTED ALMONDS
- 35 G / 1 OZ / 3 TBSP SULTANAS OR RAISINS
- 35 G / 1 OZ / 4 TBSP PINE-NUTS
- 1 MEDIUM-SIZED ONION
- PINCH OF POWDERED SAFFRON
- WHITE FLOUR
- SALT AND PEPPER
♦

PREPARATION TIME: 3 HOURS

CLEAN THE FENNEL LEAVES and boil in salted water. Drain and reserve the cooking water for boiling the pasta in. Clean the sardines, removing the head and backbone, opening them out flat. In a wide, deep-sided pan, sauté the chopped onion with the anchovies, crushing them with a fork until they dissolve. Add the sultanas, pine-nuts and a pinch of saffron, throw in the chopped fennel leaves, half the sardines and season with ground black pepper.

Cook over gentle heat, stirring from time to time until the sauce has a fair consistency.

Top up the fennel cooking water to boil the bucatini, checking the salt first.

When the pasta is cooked, add a pinch of saffron to the water. Drain and mix the pasta with two parts of the sauce. Turn into a baking tin or dish which has been oiled and crumbed.

Heat the remaining sauce, adding a little oil and the other half of the sardines. Cover the pasta with this sauce.

Scatter over the chopped, toasted almonds. Bake in a hot oven for about 10 minutes to blend the flavours.

VARIATION: you may add all the sardine sauce to the pasta without baking it. Leave a few sardines aside (about ten) to be dipped in flour and fried. Use to garnish the serving dish and then distribute them among all the dinner plates. This is the island's most famous pasta dish.

PASTA CON RAGÙ DELLA FESTA
MACARONI WITH SPECIAL MEAT SAUCE

◆

- 500 G / 1 LB HOME-MADE MACARONI OR RIGATONI
- 500 G / 1 LB FALSOMAGRO OR STUFFED MEAT ROLL (SEE PAGE 127 IN MEAT CHAP.)
- 500 G / 1 LB POTATOES
- 500 G / 1 LB PEAS
- 3-4 MEAT BALLS PER HEAD (SEE PAGE 131 IN MEAT CHAP.)
- 2 SAUSAGES (ABOUT 80 G /3 OZ EACH) PER HEAD
- 2 MEDIUM-SIZED ONIONS
- 2 BAY LEAVES
- 1 TBSP TOMATO CONCENTRATE
- SPRIG OF PARSLEY
- SPRIG OF BASIL
- 1 TBSP LARD OR 2 TBSP OLIVE OIL
- 1 MARROW BONE
- 125 ML / 8 TBSP RED WINE
- SALT
- PEPPER

◆

PREPARATION TIME: 3 HOURS

Sauté the chopped onion in a little oil in a large, preferably earthenware saucepan. Add the parsley, the bay leaves, the tomato concentrate dissolved in hot water, and the bone with its marrow. Simmer for about 20 minutes. Heat the lard or oil in another saucepan and brown the "falsomagro", the meat balls, the sausages and the potatoes cut into small chunks. Put the rolled meat in the saucepan with the tomato sauce and cook for about 30 minutes. Add the sausages and, after 20 minutes, throw in the potatoes (careful not to overcook) and add the peas. Remove the potatoes first of all from the sauce and put aside, then the sausage and the "falsamagro", which you will leave to cool before slipping off the string and slicing. Arrange the meat slices in the centre of a large serving dish and align the sausages and meat balls to form a crown, with the potatoes forming the outermost ring. Pour some of the sauce with the peas over the "falsomagro" slices. Keep the platter hot in the oven or over a saucepan of hot water for serving as the second course.

Meanwhile, cook the home-made macaroni (or rigatoni), drain when "al dente", arrange on a serving dish, pour the sauce with the peas over and serve immediately.

PASTA CON SUGO PICCANTE
PASTA WITH A PIQUANT SAUCE

◆

- 500 G / 1 LB BUCATINI (PASTA STRAWS)
- 1 KG / 2 LBS TOMATOES
- 500 G / 1 LB ONIONS
- 100 G / 4 OZ / ⅔ CUP BLACK OLIVES
- 4 ANCHOVY FILLETS
- 1 CLOVE OF GARLIC
- BASIL
- OREGANO
- HOT RED PEPPER

◆

PREPARATION TIME: 30 MINUTES

IN A LITTLE OIL IN A SAUCEPAN, sauté a clove of garlic (to be removed as soon as it colours), the anchovy and chopped onion. Add the skinned and seeded tomatoes, roughly chopped, the pitted black olives, the basil and the oregano. Blend the flavours well over gentle heat. Boil the bucatini in plenty of salted water, drain while still firm and pour the sauce over. Hand the hot red pepper round the table for those who like it.

THE NAME "CANNIZZI" derives from the fact that the bucatini were made at home by using a rod or "cane" of dry wheat which was pulled out when the pasta had dried.

PASTA CON SUGO E CARCIOFI RIPIENI
SPAGHETTI WITH TOMATO SAUCE AND STUFFED ARTICHOKES

◆

- 500 G / 1 LB SPAGHETTI
- 1 KG / 2 LBS RIPE TOMATOES
- 6 GLOBE ARTICHOKES
- 4 CLOVES OF GARLIC
- 2 ONIONS
- 2 ANCHOVY FILLETS
- 1 EGG
- BASIL
- PARSLEY
- DRY BREADCRUMBS
- GRATED PECORINO CHEESE
- SALT AND PEPPER

◆

PREPARATION TIME: 1½ HOURS

IN A LARGE SAUCEPAN, put the roughly-chopped tomatoes, the onion, two cloves of garlic, the basil and salt. Cook for about twenty minutes. Put through a "mouli légumes" and return to the pan. In a little oil in another pan, dissolve the anchovy and colour the dry breadcrumbs in it. Allow to cool, then add the grated cheese, pepper and chopped parsley and garlic.

Remove the tough outer leaves from the artichokes and discard all spiky parts. Open out the leaves and press the dry breadcrumb filling between them. Beat the egg in a soup plate and dip the artichokes in it. Allow the egg on the artichokes to set in a little oil in a frying pan, thus making a bung to hold the stuffing in.

Heat the sauce and lay the artichokes on top, upside down. Cook gently for half-an-hour.

Boil the spaghetti, drain "al dente" and serve with the tomato sauce. The artichokes accompany the second course.

PASTA CON SUGO DI TONNO
SPAGHETTI WITH TUNA SAUCE

- 500 G / 1 LB SPAGHETTI
- 500 G / 1 LB RIPE TOMATOES OR A TIN (CAN) SKINNED TOMATOES (2½ CUPS)
- 250 G / ½ LB TINNED (CANNED) TUNA IN OLIVE OIL (1¼ CUPS)
- 3 ANCHOVY FILLETS
- 2 CLOVES OF GARLIC
- PINCH OF OREGANO
- SPRIG OF PARSLEY
- HOT RED PEPPER

PREPARATION TIME: 30 MINUTES

SAUTÉ THE CHOPPED GARLIC in a little oil in a saucepan, together with the anchovy that you will crush with a fork. Add the tomato pulp and a pinch of oregano and simmer gently for 10 minutes.

Add the tuna and allow the flavours to develop for another 5 minutes. Before drawing off the heat, add the chopped parsley. Boil the spaghetti, drain "al dente" and pour the sauce over. Pass the hot red pepper round separately.

VARIATION: you can prepare an excellent sauce by using the same ingredients, but without the tomato. In this case, I advise you to double the quantity of tuna - you will need 500 g (1 lb) in all.

PASTA CON SUGO E RICOTTA
SPAGHETTI WITH TOMATO SAUCE AND RICOTTA

- 500 G / 1 LB SPAGHETTI
- 1 KG / 2 LBS RIPE TOMATOES
- 500 G / 1 LB / 2¾ CUPS RICOTTA
- 100 G / 4 OZ / 1 CUP GRATED PECORINO OR PARMESAN CHEESE
- 2 ONIONS
- BASIL
- SALT
- BLACK PEPPER

PREPARATION TIME: 45 MINUTES

PREPARE THE SAUCE by putting the roughly-chopped tomatoes and onions, the basil and the salt in a saucepan. Cook until the liquid has all evaporated. Pass the sauce through a "mouli légumes" and season with pepper and olive oil. Boil the pasta in plenty of salted water. Remove with the aid of a long-handled fork and place in a bowl where you will have meanwhile dissolved the ricotta with a little of the pasta cooking water, crushing it with a fork. Sprinkle with grated cheese, cover with the sauce and mix well.

THIS IS CONSIDERED a typically spring-time dish, boding well for a fine summer.

PASTA CON VONGOLE FRESCHE
SPAGHETTI WITH FRESH CLAMS

- 500 G / 1 LB SPAGHETTI
- 500 G / 1 LB / 2 GENEROUS CUPS SHELLED BABY CLAMS
- 4 ANCHOVY FILLETS
- 2 CLOVES OF GARLIC
- SPRIG OF PARSLEY
- 125 ML / 4 FL OZ / ½ CUP DRY WHITE WINE
- SALT
- PEPPER OR HOT RED PEPPER
- OLIVE OIL

PREPARATION TIME: 30 MINUTES

SAUTÉ THE GARLIC, chopped, in some oil in a saucepan, together with the anchovies, crushed with a fork. Add the clams and cook for about 10 minutes. Sprinkle over the wine. Once evaporated, add the parsley, the pepper or hot red pepper and turn off the heat. Boil the spaghetti in plenty of salted water, drain while still "al dente", turn into a serving bowl and serve with the sauce.

VARIATION: 500 g (1 lb) ripe tomatoes, skinned, seeded and roughly-chopped, may be added after the wine has evaporated. They must cook for at least 5 minutes. Never serve cheese with clams.

PASTA CON VONGOLE E COZZE
SPAGHETTI WITH CLAMS AND MUSSELS

- 500 G / 1 LB SPAGHETTI
- 500 G / 1 LB BABY CLAMS IN THEIR SHELLS
- 500 G / 1 LB MUSSELS IN THEIR SHELLS
- 3 CLOVES OF GARLIC, CHOPPED
- SPRIG OF PARSLEY, CHOPPED
- HOT RED PEPPER

PREPARATION TIME: 1 HOUR

WASH THE MUSSELS and clams thoroughly under running water. Put a little water in a saucepan, bring to the boil and throw in the shellfish. Cook until the shells have opened, then take them out, reserving their liquor. Remove the flesh from the shells, leaving a dozen or so intact for decorating the serving dish with. Sauté the garlic in a frying pan (better if it is an earthenware pot), add the shellfish, season with salt and pepper and cook for 15 minutes. Just before turning off the heat, add the chopped parsley. Boil the spaghetti in the shellfish cooking water, drain while still "al dente" and transfer to the frying pan or earthenware pot. Stir well and serve in a terracotta bowl. Garnish with the clams and mussels that you have put aside and serve the hot red pepper separately for those who like it.

PASTA CON ZUCCHINE FRITTE

SPAGHETTI WITH FRIED COURGETTES

◆

- 500 G / 1 LB SPAGHETTI
- 4 COURGETTES (ZUCCHINI)
- 2 CLOVES OF GARLIC
- GRATED PECORINO OR PARMESAN CHEESE
- SALT
- PEPPER
- OLIVE OIL

◆

PREPARATION TIME: 45 MINUTES

CUT THE COURGETTES into rings and fry in hot oil which has been flavoured with 2 cloves of garlic, removed when golden. Boil the spaghetti, drain while still resistant to the tooth and turn into a bowl.

Dress with the courgettes and the frying oil. Pass pepper and some grated cheese round separately.

This is a classic summer dish, especially in the Palermo area.

102

PASTA E PISELLI
SPAGHETTI WITH PEAS

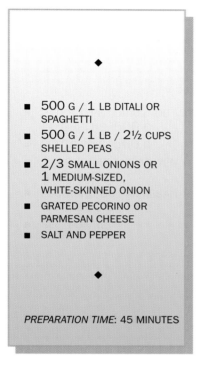

- 500 G / 1 LB DITALI OR SPAGHETTI
- 500 G / 1 LB / 2½ CUPS SHELLED PEAS
- 2/3 SMALL ONIONS OR 1 MEDIUM-SIZED, WHITE-SKINNED ONION
- GRATED PECORINO OR PARMESAN CHEESE
- SALT AND PEPPER

PREPARATION TIME: 45 MINUTES

CHOP THE ONION and sauté in some oil in a saucepan. Add the shelled peas, stir well, season with salt and pour a glass of water over. Leave to cook over a low flame for 20 minutes. Boil the spaghetti, drain while still "al dente" and turn into a serving bowl. Add the peas, season with pepper and serve at table, passing the grated cheese round separately. This is a spring-time dish, when the peas are sweet and tender. If you increase the amounts and break in some eggs, you may serve it as a main course.

PASTA FRITTA
FRIED PASTA

- 500 G / 1 LB CAPELLI D'ANGELO OR VERY FINE SPAGHETTI
- 3 EGGS
- 150 G / 6 OZ / ½ CUP HONEY
- 100 G / 4 OZ / 1 CUP DRY BREADCRUMBS
- OLIVE OIL

PREPARATION TIME: 45 MINUTES

BOIL THE PASTA in salted water and drain. Beat the eggs with salt and pepper in one bowl and turn the breadcrumbs into another. Add the pasta to the bowl containing the egg, stirring well. Then transfer to the bowl with the breadcrumbs. Heat some oil in a saucepan and when it is hot, gently slip in the pasta. Once a crust has formed, turn it all over. When ready, transfer to some kitchen paper, helping yourself with a spatula. Remove the paper and pour over the honey dissolved in half a glass of water and serve.

VARIATION: you may also add 50 g (2 oz / ½ cup) dry breadcrumbs to the bowl where you beat the eggs with the salt and pepper. In this case, the pasta must be served without the honey.

PASTA SFIZIOSA
PASTA CAPRICE

- 500 G / 1 LB SPAGHETTI
- 500 G / 1 LB RIPE TOMATOES OR 2½ CUPS PREPARED TOMATO PULP
- 50 G / 2 OZ / ⅓ CUP PITTED (STONED) GREEN OLIVES
- 25 G / 1 OZ / 2 TBSP PICKLED CAPERS
- 3 ANCHOVY FILLETS
- 2 CLOVES OF GARLIC
- 2 PICKLED GHERKINS
- OREGANO
- BASIL

PREPARATION TIME: 45 MINUTES

IN A LITTLE OIL, sauté the chopped garlic with the anchovies, the gherkins cut into rings, the capers and the olives. Add the tomato pulp, season with salt and pepper and cook for about 30 minutes over gentle heat.

Boil the pasta in salted water, drain and place on a serving dish. Pour on the sauce and sprinkle with basil and oregano.

VARIATION: try substituting the green olives with big, fleshy black ones. Add a little finely-chopped parsley, garlic and hot red pepper.

RISO CON LE CASTAGNE
RICE WITH CHESTNUTS

- 500 G / 1 LB / 2 CUPS LONG-GRAIN RICE
- 500 G / 1 LB / 2 ⅔ CUPS DRIED CHESTNUTS
- 6 ANCHOVY FILLETS
- 1 TBSP TOMATO PASTE
- 1 SMALL TIN (CAN) TOMATO CONCENTRATE
- 1 WHITE-SKINNED ONION
- SALT
- PEPPER
- OLIVE OIL

PREPARATION TIME: 45 MINUTES

PUT THE DRIED CHESTNUTS to soak overnight. Brown the chopped onion in a little oil in a saucepan, add the tomato concentrate dissolved in a glass of hot water and throw in the drained chestnuts. Cover with water and season with salt and pepper. Simmer for 1 hour. Boil the rice in salted water, drain while the grains are still firm and add to the saucepan of chestnuts.

While the rice is cooking, dissolve the anchovies in some oil in a small pan; this will be used to flavour the chestnut rice.

THIS IS ONE of the Palermo district's most ancient poor man's dishes. There is another area in Sicily, precisely at Lipari, where the dish is very similar to the one typical of Pollina. The cooking method is the same, except pasta is used instead of rice.

TIMBALLO DI RISO
RICE TIMBALE

- 1 KG / 2 LBS / 4 CUPS LONG-GRAIN RICE
- 600 G / 1½ LB MINCED (GROUND) MEAT
- 500 G / 1 LB / 2¼ CUPS SHELLED PEAS
- 200 G / 8 OZ PRIMOSALE CHEESE
- 150 G / 6 OZ / 1½ CUPS GRATED CACIOCAVALLO OR PARMESAN CHEESE
- 2 EGGS
- 2 ONIONS
- 2 CLOVES OF GARLIC
- 1 SMALL TIN (CAN) TOMATO CONCENTRATE
- 1 GENEROUS TBSP TOMATO PASTE
- 125 ML / 4 FL OZ / ½ CUP DRY WHITE WINE
- SALAMI
- BASIL
- CINNAMON AND GRANULATED SUGAR

PREPARATION TIME: 1½ HOURS

BROWN THE CHOPPED ONION and the whole garlic (to be removed as soon as it colours). Add the minced meat, stir and pour the white wine on after a few minutes. Allow to evaporate and pour in the tomato concentrate, dissolved in a cup of hot water. Add the salt and pepper and aromatise with the chopped basil. Cook for about 30 minutes. Add the peas and continue cooking for about 15 minutes. Meanwhile, cook the rice in salted water and drain while still firm. Fill a small bowl with plain rice and set aside. Dress the rice with two thirds of the grated cheese and the tomato sauce. Arrange half of the rice in an oiled baking tin or ovenproof dish and place slices of primosale and salami on top. Cover with the other half of the rice. Beat the egg with the rest of the caciocavallo, a pinch of cinnamon and a teaspoon of sugar. Pour the mixture into the bowl of plain rice, stir and pour onto the timbale to make the final layer. Bake in a hot oven for about 20 minutes. The name derives from Thummel, the Arab emir who lived in Sicily for a long time.

TIMBALLO DI RISO CON LE MELANZANE
RICE TIMBALE WITH AUBERGINES

- 500 G / 1 LB / 2 CUPS LONG-GRAIN RICE
- 1 KG / 2 LBS RIPE TOMATOES
- 150 G / 6 OZ PRIMOSALE CHEESE
- 50 G / 2 OZ PECORINO CHEESE
- 4 AUBERGINES (EGGPLANTS)
- 1 ONION
- POWDERED SAFFRON
- BASIL AND PARSLEY

PREPARATION TIME: 2 HOURS

SLICE THE AUBERGINES and put to soak for an hour in salted water. Squeeze them, dry in kitchen paper and fry in hot oil. Sauté the chopped onion in a saucepan, skin the tomatoes, discard their seeds and roughly chop. Add the onion with the chopped basil and parsley, season with salt and pepper and cook gently for about 30 minutes. Boil the rice in salted water and dissolve a pinch of saffron powder in it. Oil a baking dish, make a layer of rice and cover it with the sauce, the fried aubergines and a few slices of primosale. Repeat the layers until all the ingredients have been used up. Dredge with grated pecorino cheese and bake in the oven for 20 minutes. Before serving, sprinkle with chopped basil and parsley.

TIMBALLO DI RISO DELLA CUCINA BARONALE

BARONIAL RICE TIMBALE

♦

- 1 KG / 2 LBS / 4 CUPS LONG-GRAIN RICE
- BOILING FOWL
- 500 G / 1 LB MINCED (GROUND) MEAT
- 200 G / 8 OZ SAUSAGES
- 300 G / 12 OZ / 3 CUPS GRATED PECORINO OR PARMESAN CHEESE
- 100 G / 4 OZ PRIMOSALE OR MILD PROVOLA CHEESE
- 100 G / 4 OZ FRESH CACIOCAVALLO OR SARDINIAN OR TUSCAN CACIOTTA OR SHARP PROVOLA CHEESE
- 3 EGGS
- 2 TBSP TOMATO EXTRACT OR 1 SMALL TIN (CAN) TOMATO CONCENTRATE
- 2 MEDIUM-SIZED ONIONS
- 2 RIPE TOMATOES
- 2 CHOPPED CLOVES OF GARLIC
- SPRIG OF PARSLEY
- STICK OF CELERY
- PINCH OF CINNAMON
- PINCH OF GRANULATED SUGAR
- 125 ML / 4 FL OZ / ½ CUP MILK
- DRY BREADCRUMBS
- OLIVE OIL OR LARD

♦

PREPARATION TIME: 4 HOURS

BOIL THE CHICKEN with an onion, two tomatoes, a sprig of parsley and the stick of celery. Mix the minced meat with the grated pecorino cheese, an egg, the garlic, 50 g (2 oz / ½ cup) dry breadcrumbs, the milk, salt and pepper. Make about 40 small meat balls, 20 of which you will put in the chicken stock and the other half you will fry in the oil or lard in a frying pan where you will also fry the skinned sausages. Sauté the chopped onion in a saucepan and add the tomato concentrate dissolved in hot water. Put the fried meat balls and sausagemeat in the sauce and cook over a moderate flame for 20 minutes.

When the chicken is well-cooked, remove from its broth and allow to cool. Skin and bone it, cut up the flesh and put aside together with the meat balls. Filter the broth and return to the heat. Check for salt, top up with water and cook the rice. Drain while the grains are still firm. Pour on the sauce and the grated cheese.

Oil and crumb a deep-sided baking dish, arrange the first layer of rice, add a layer of meat balls, pieces of chicken and slices of primosale. Make another layer of rice, place the meat balls with their sauce on top, cover with the sausage meat and crumble the caciocavallo over.

Cover with a final layer of rice, mixed in with the remaining pieces of chicken and meat. Finally pour on a sauce made of eggs, beaten with 50 g (2 oz / 6 tbsp) grated cheese, a pinch of cinnamon, a tablespoon of sugar, salt and pepper. Bake in a hot oven for 30 minutes.

VARIATION: this dish may be eaten cold. Or it may be put into an oiled baking dish, cut into rectangles, dressed with skinned, roughly-chopped tomatoes, stoned black olives, a few anchovy fillets and olive oil, and heated through for 10 minutes.

SAUCES

"Nun c'è megghiu sarsa di la fami"
(There is no better sauce than hunger)

E. Alaimo *"Proverbi Siciliani" Edit. Martello*

The sauces for serving with pasta are described in all the recipes in the chapter on pasta dishes. I wish here to repeat the simplest recipe for fresh tomato sauce that forms the core for a great number of dishes. Prepared in the summer, this sauce is preserved in glass jars to be consumed during the winter.

The sauces presented in this chapter are condiments for boiled or grilled meat and fish. In the daily fare of the common folk, sauces were not contemplated for boiled meat and fish dishes - the only dressing was olive oil and lemon or pickles. I have chosen to give the recipes for sauces used in the "monsù" cuisine where the ability in preparing them can be expressed. Indeed, it was the French who introduced their sauces based on olive oil, garlic, lemon and oregano and, in the more sophisticated dishes, almonds, pine-nuts, olives, capers, etc. These sauces are quick and simple to make and enhance dishes with their colour and flavour.

Once you begin to make them, your guests will show immense gratitude.

AGLIATA
GARLIC SAUCE

- ◆ -

- ■ 4-5 CLOVES OF GARLIC
- ■ 125 ML / 4 FL OZ / ½ CUP OF WHITE WINE VINEGAR
- ■ OLIVE OIL

- ◆ -

PREPARATION TIME: 5 MINUTES

SAUTÉ THE GARLIC (broken into two or three pieces or else chopped) in hot oil in a little pan. Pour in the vinegar, allow to evaporate for 2 minutes and draw off the heat. This sauce is particularly suitable with fried blue-fish.

SALSA DI CIPOLLA CON L'ACETO
ONION AND VINEGAR SAUCE

- ◆ -

- ■ 1 ONION
- ■ 60 ML / 2 FL OZ / ¼ CUP VINEGAR
- ■ PARSLEY
- ■ SALT AND PEPPER
- ■ OLIVE OIL

- ◆ -

PREPARATION TIME: 15 MINUTES

CHOP THE ONION and sweat in a little oil without frying. Add half a glass of hot water. When it has evaporated, sprinkle the vinegar over. Give this 2-3 minutes to evaporate and pour the sauce over tuna fish or fried salted cod.

SALSA DI MANDORLE
ALMOND SAUCE

◆

- 1 LARGE ONION
- 25 G / 1 OZ / 2½ TBSP GREEN OLIVES
- 10 G / 1 OZ / 2 TBSP CAPERS
- 2 RIPE TOMATOES
- 2 ANCHOVY FILLETS
- 25 G / 1 OZ / 4 TBSP CHOPPED AND TOASTED ALMONDS
- 25G / 1 OZ / 2 TBSP GRANULATED SUGAR
- 25 G / 1 OZ / 3 TBSP WHITE FLOUR
- 60 ML / 2 FL OZ / ¼ CUP VINEGAR

◆

PREPARATION TIME: 30 MINUTES

I N A LITTLE OLIVE OIL in an earthenware pot, brown the roughly-chopped onions, the anchovies broken into little pieces, the flour and the almonds, olives and capers chopped up together, along with the skinned, seeded and roughly-chopped tomatoes. Stir and cook for 10 minutes. Before turning off the heat, sprinkle with sugar and vinegar and allow to evaporate for 2 or 3 minutes.

This sauce is excellent served with boiled fish.

SALSA DI MENTA
MINT SAUCE

◆

- 60 ML / 2 FL OZ / ¼ CUP VINEGAR
- SALT
- PEPPER
- OLIVE OIL

◆

PREPARATION TIME: 15 MINUTES

P UT THE OIL, vinegar, salt and pepper in a little bowl. Blend well with a fork and add the finely-chopped mint. Stir well and serve this sauce with boiled meat.

SALSA DI SEMI DI PAPAVERO
POPPY SEED SAUCE

- ■ 100 G / 4 OZ / 1 CUP TOASTED ALMONDS
- ■ 50 G / 2 OZ / ½ CUP DRY BREADCRUMBS
- ■ 2 CLOVES OF GARLIC
- ■ 15 G / ½ OZ / 1 TSP POPPY SEEDS
- ■ 1 BOILED POTATO
- ■ 1 SPRIG PARSLEY, CHOPPED
- ■ 60 ML / 2 FL OZ / ¼ CUP VINEGAR
- ■ HOT RED PEPPER
- ■ OLIVE OIL AND SALT

PREPARATION TIME: 20 MINUTES

POUND THE GARLIC, almonds, parsley, poppy seeds and the potato in a mortar (today an electric chopper or food processor can be used).

Transfer to a bowl and add the oil, alternated with the vinegar, stirring all the time, until the sauce becomes soft and thick. Excellent for boiled meat and fish.

SALSA DI POMODORO
HOME-MADE TOMATO SAUCE

- ■ 1 KG RIPE TOMATOES
- ■ 2 LARGE ONIONS
- ■ 5-6 BASIL LEAVES
- ■ SALT
- ■ PEPPER OR HOT RED PEPPER
- ■ OLIVE OIL

PREPARATION TIME: 15 MINUTES

PLACE THE ROUGHLY-CHOPPED TOMATOES and onions in a saucepan and add the basil and salt. Cook for 30 minutes. Put through a "mouli lègumes" (food mill) and season with uncooked olive oil and pepper or hot red pepper.

THIS SAUCE is the basic one which we used to make in my family not just for serving over spaghetti or other types of pasta, but also for masking excellent main dishes such as meat balls, stuffed vegetables, egg dishes, etc. There are various variations to this sauce: it can be made by first frying the onion and/or garlic, or else with herbs and the most imaginative condiments. Furthermore, it varies from family to family. Indeed, to take away the acidity of the tomatoes, some families add bicarbonate of soda and others sugar. In any case, tomato sauce is the sauce par excellence.

SALSA MARINARA
FISH SAUCE

◆

- 500 G / 1 LB FISH TRIMMINGS: BONES AND HEADS
- 25 G / 1 OZ / 3 TBSP WHITE FLOUR
- PARSLEY SPRIG
- BAY LEAF
- 1 LEMON
- 2 EGG YOLKS
- 125 ML / 4 FL OZ / ½ CUP WHITE WINE
- 1 ONION
- FEW THYME LEAVES
- SALT AND PEPPER

◆

PREPARATION TIME: 1 HOUR

WASH THE FISH TRIMMINGS and cook for 30 minutes in a saucepan with water, parsley stalks, half the onion, the bay leaf, thyme, half the wine and salt. Filter the stock and keep hot over gentle heat. Chop the remaining onion which you will sauté in a pan with the oil, adding the flour and stirring with a wooden spoon. Pour over the remaining wine and leave to evaporate before adding the hot fish stock. Cook for 15 minutes, stirring constantly. Sprinkle over the parsley, two beaten egg yolks and lemon juice and draw off the heat. This sauce is excellent with boiled fish.

HERE IS A SAUCE concocted with what usually gets thrown away - the fish heads and bones (cleaned before being cooked). The aristocracy appreciated their own monsu's brand of micro-economy and showed his culinary skill off with pride to guests.

SALSA PANE E AGLIO
BREAD AND GARLIC SAUCE

◆

- 2 TBSP DRY BREADCRUMBS
- 2-3 CLOVES OF GARLIC
- 60 ML / 4 TBSP BROTH
- 1 TBSP VINEGAR
- PEPPER OR HOT RED PEPPER
- SALT
- OLIVE OIL

◆

PREPARATION TIME: 15 MINUTES

MOISTEN THE DRY BREADCRUMBS in the broth, season with salt and pepper (or hot red pepper), the chopped garlic, a trickle of olive oil and the vinegar. Stir well and serve. This sauce accompanies cold boiled meat.

VARIAION: for a stronger, more flavoursome sauce, toast the breadcrumbs slightly with two anchovy fillets in a little oil in a saucepan. Proceed to work the sauce as above.
It was precisely by means of these small additions and cooking procedures that the cook made an effort to impress the guests.

SALSA SARACENA
SARACENIC SAUCE

◆

- **200** G / **8** OZ / **1⅓** CUPS PITTED (STONED) GREEN OLIVES
- **3** ANCHOVY FILLETS
- **25** G / **1** OZ / **3** TBSP WHITE FLOUR
- **20** G / ¾ OZ / **2** TBSP SULTANAS OR RAISINS
- **20** G / ¾ OZ / **3** TBSP PINE-NUTS
- **1** SACHET OF POWDERED SAFFRON
- PINCH OREGANO

◆

PREPARATION TIME: 15 MINUTES

SALSA SFIZIOSA
SAUCE CAPRICE

◆

- SPRIG OF PARSLEY
- **1** CELERY HEART
- **1** SMALL ONION
- **2** ANCHOVY FILLETS
- **2** PICKLED GHERKINS
- **30** G / **1** OZ / **2** TBSP PICKLED CAPERS
- GRATED ZEST AND JUICE OF **1** LEMON
- GRATED ZEST OF **1** ORANGE
- SALT AND PEPPER

◆

PREPARATION TIME: 20 MINUTES

DISSOLVE THE ANCHOVY in a little oil in a saucepan (or rather an earthenware pot), add the olives, capers, sultanas and pine-nuts, all chopped up together. Mix the flour and saffron to a smooth paste with half a glass of hot water in a cup, pour into the pan, stir well and leave to blend for 5-10 minutes.

This sauce is excellent with boiled beef or chicken.

CHOP THE HERBS with the anchovies, gherkins, capers and the grated lemon and orange zest .

Mix well, alternating olive oil and lemon juice until you have obtained a thick, smooth sauce. Season with salt and pepper and serve with boiled fish.

SALSA VERDE
GREEN SAUCE

♦

- 30 G / 1 OZ / 2 TBSP CAPERS
- 3 ANCHOVY FILLETS
- 2-3 BASIL LEAVES
- ¼ ONION OR 1 SPRING ONION (SCALLION)
- 1 LEMON
- 1 HARD-BOILED EGG YOLK
- HANDFUL CHOPPED PARSLEY
- OLIVE OIL

♦

PREPARATION TIME: 20 MINUTES

CHOP UP THE CAPERS, anchovy, onion, basil, parsley and egg yolk in the food chopper. Add the olive oil, alternated with the lemon juice, continuing to blend until the sauce is nice and smooth.

This is excellent served with boiled meat. I advise you to get the sauce ready a few hours beforehand.

MEAT

"Carni e pisci, la vita ti crisci"
(Your life-span increases if you eat meat and fish)

E. Alaimo *"Proverbi Siciliani"* Edit. Martello

Meat-based second courses were for feast days, for growing children and for convalescents who had to regain their physical strength. There was not a great number of such dishes and the meat was proverbially tough, because the animals were exploited to the utmost for work in the fields before being sent to the slaughterhouse. Besides, the pasturage consisted of dry grass for many months in the year. The dishes most commonly found throughout Sicily were, accordingly, based on minced meat: meat balls, meat rolls, forcemeat.

On special occasions, calves were butchered so that dishes such as "falsomagro", "agglassatu", etc. could be prepared....

In certain periods of the year, lambs, chicken, pigs, rabbits and game were used in tasty dishes. Lamb was consumed at Easter, pork at Christmas and game when the animals passed through the territory.

AGNELLO IN UMIDO
STEWED LAMB

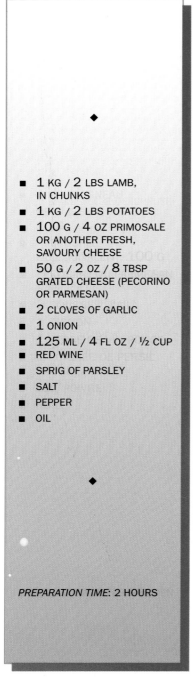

- 1 KG / 2 LBS LAMB, IN CHUNKS
- 1 KG / 2 LBS POTATOES
- 100 G / 4 OZ PRIMOSALE OR ANOTHER FRESH, SAVOURY CHEESE
- 50 G / 2 OZ / 8 TBSP GRATED CHEESE (PECORINO OR PARMESAN)
- 2 CLOVES OF GARLIC
- 1 ONION
- 125 ML / 4 FL OZ / ½ CUP RED WINE
- SPRIG OF PARSLEY
- SALT
- PEPPER
- OIL

PREPARATION TIME: 2 HOURS

TAKE A FRYING PAN (or preferably an earthenware pot) and sauté the chopped onion in a little oil, adding the garlic and parsley chopped up together and the chunks of meat. Turn to brown all over, pour on the red wine and cover with the lid.

Peel and cut up the potatoes, add to the lamb, season with salt and pepper and replace the lid. Continue cooking over gentle heat for about an hour.

Before serving, flavour with the sliced primosale and dredge with the grated cheese.

Some of the sauce may be used with pasta.

ARROSTO DI MAIALE AL LIMONE

LEMON-FLAVOURED PORK

- 800 G / 1¾ LBS LOIN OF PORK
- 3 LEMONS
- 1 KG / 2 LBS POTATOES (NEW ONES IF IN SEASON)
- 5 TBSP VEGETABLE OIL
- 10 WHITE PEPPERCORNS
- 1 CLOVE OF GARLIC
- ROSEMARY
- BAY LEAF
- WHITE FLOUR
- SALT

PREPARATION TIME: 1½ HOURS

COAT THE LOIN OF PORK in flour and sear in the oil in a meat tin (baking pan) with all the herbs and garlic. Add the peeled, finely-sliced potatoes and season with salt and pepper. Add the juice of three lemons, the grated zest of one lemon and a glass of water.

Roast in a hot oven for about an hour.

— 119 —

BOLLITO DI CARNE

BOILED MEAT

- ◆
- 1 KG / 2 LBS BRISKET OF BEEF
- 2 TOMATOES
- 2 ONIONS
- 2 POTATOES
- 1 MARROW BONE
- BAY LEAF
- A FEW PEPPERCORNS
- 1 STICK OF CELERY
- BUNCH OF PARSLEY
- SALT
- ◆

PREPARATION TIME: 3-4 HOURS

PUT COLD WATER to cover the meat in a saucepan, along with the parsley, celery, peppercorns, bay leaf and the tomatoes, skinned, seeded and roughly chopped. As soon as the water begins to boil, skim the surface and add the onions whole. Continue to cook for about 2 hours. Add the potatoes and cook a further hour over moderate heat.

MINT SAUCE is the classical accompaniment to boiled meat and is prepared many hours before it is needed. This is how to make it: emulsify some olive oil and vinegar, season with salt and pepper and pour the liquid onto the mint leaves. Mix well and leave to rest for as long as possible.

Here are the ingredients:
2 TABLESPOONS OLIVE OIL
SALT
PEPPER
A HANDFUL OF MINT LEAVES
60 ML / 2 FL OZ / ¼ CUP VINEGAR

CAPRETTO AL FORNO CON PATATE
ROAST KID WITH POTATOES

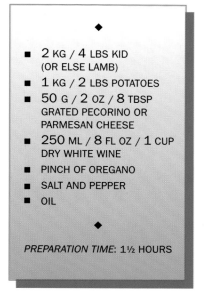

- 2 KG / 4 LBS KID (OR ELSE LAMB)
- 1 KG / 2 LBS POTATOES
- 50 G / 2 OZ / 8 TBSP GRATED PECORINO OR PARMESAN CHEESE
- 250 ML / 8 FL OZ / 1 CUP DRY WHITE WINE
- PINCH OF OREGANO
- SALT AND PEPPER
- OIL

PREPARATION TIME: 1½ HOURS

PLACE THE POTATOES cut into chunks in an oiled baking tin or dish and season with salt and pepper, oregano and oil. Add the pieces of kid, season again with salt and pepper, pour over the white wine and roast in a hot oven for an hour. Before turning off the oven once the meat is cooked, sprinkle some grated cheese over.

KID IS A CLASSICAL EASTER DISH. The way it is prepared differs from zone to zone, and even within the same family there may be variations, with the addition of some aromatic herb or some other ingredient. The classical Easter dish eaten in the countryside was charcoal-grilled kid or lamb, drenched in olive oil aromatised with various herbs and brushed on unstintingly with a twig of rosemary.

CAPRETTO AL VINO ROSSO
ROAST KID IN RED WINE

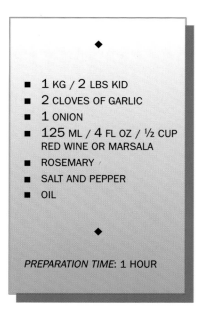

- 1 KG / 2 LBS KID
- 2 CLOVES OF GARLIC
- 1 ONION
- 125 ML / 4 FL OZ / ½ CUP RED WINE OR MARSALA
- ROSEMARY
- SALT AND PEPPER
- OIL

PREPARATION TIME: 1 HOUR

IN A RATHER LARGE SAUCEPAN (preferably an earthenware pot), brown the chopped onion and the whole garlic cloves in a little oil. When coloured, add the pieces of meat. Sauté carefully, cover with hot water and continue cooking over slow heat. Once a dense gravy has formed, add salt, pepper and a glass of Marsala which you will allow to evaporate before turning off the heat.

THIS WAS an Easter dish for well-off families. Red wine was used to cover the strong caprine flavour and because, as my grandmother would say, it made the dish more digestible.

CAPRETTO CON STRACCIATELLA
KID WITH EGG AND CHEESE BROTH

- 1 KG / 2 LBS KID
- 5 EGGS
- 2 ONIONS
- 100 G / 4 OZ / 1 CUP GRATED PECORINO OR PARMESAN CHEESE
- SPRIG OF PARSLEY, CHOPPED
- SALT AND PEPPER
- OIL

PREPARATION TIME: 2 HOURS

IN A RATHER LARGE SAUCEPAN (preferably an earthenware pot), brown the chopped onion in a little oil. Add the pieces of meat and, when golden, season with salt, pepper and chopped parsley. Cover with hot water and continue to cook over a slow flame for about an hour. Meanwhile, with a fork, beat the eggs in a bowl, together with the grated cheese, salt and pepper. Pour onto the kid and stir. If the gravy is too dry, add a little hot water. Keep over the heat for another 5 minutes before drawing it off.

The gravy can also be used as a sauce for pasta.

THIS EASTER DISH is found in the eastern area of Sicily. It is a dish for well-to-do families because the portions of kid do not have much meat in them. One kilogram of kid is enough for six people. The side-plate is usually a fry-up of mixed vegetables.

CARNE IMPANATA CON L'ORIGANO
BREADED BEEF WITH OREGANO

- 500 G / 1 LB BEEF SLICES
- 70 G / 3 OZ / ¾ CUP DRY BREADCRUMBS
- OREGANO
- SALT AND PEPPER
- OLIVE OIL

PREPARATION TIME: 20 MINUTES

POUR A LITTLE OIL, seasoned with salt and pepper, into a bowl. In another one, put the dry breadcrumbs, mixed with oregano, salt and pepper.

Place each meat slice first into the oil and then into the breadcrumbs and oregano, and arrange in a barely-oiled baking tin or dish. Cook for 15 minutes in a hot oven.

THIS IS A QUICK, SIMPLE DISH which you can prepare while you are waiting for the pasta to cook. It is a recipe with guaranteed success as it is tasteful and pleasantly fragrant.

CONIGLIO ALL'AGRODOLCE

SWEET AND SOUR RABBIT

- ◆ -

- 1 RABBIT, JOINTED
- 200 G / 8 OZ / 1⅓ CUPS PITTED (STONED) GREEN OLIVES
- 100 G / 4 OZ / ⅔ CUP WHITE FLOUR
- 50 G / 2 OZ / ¼ CUP CAPERS
- 25 G / 1 OZ / 2 TBSP GRANULATED SUGAR
- 1 ONION
- 1 STICK OF CELERY
- 125 ML / 4 FL OZ / ½ CUP OF VINEGAR
- 125 ML / 4 FL OZ / ½ CUP WHITE WINE

- ◆ -

PREPARATION TIME: 1 HOUR

COAT THE RABBIT JOINTS in flour and fry in hot oil in a frying pan. Douse with the vinegar and sugar.

After a few minutes, once the liquid has evaporated, turn off the heat and cover the pan. Meanwhile, in a saucepan with a little oil, gently sauté the chopped onion, the celery cut into chunks, the pitted, roughly-chopped olives and the capers. Season with salt and pepper and, when it has all amalgamated, add the browned rabbit and cook for a further 20 minutes, sprinkling some white wine over if the sauce tends to dry up.

For a smoother sauce, chop up the onion, celery, olives and capers in an electric blender. The second stage of cooking may also be carried out in a hot oven.

CONIGLIO IN UMIDO CON I CARCIOFI
STEWED RABBIT WITH ARTICHOKES

- 4 HIND JOINTS OF A RABBIT
- 6 GLOBE ARTICHOKES
- BAY LEAF
- SPRIG OF ROSEMARY
- 3 CLOVES OF GARLIC
- BUNCH OF PARSLEY
- STOCK
- FLOUR
- SALT
- POWDERED HOT RED PEPPER
- OIL

PREPARATION TIME: 2 HOURS

I N A WIDE-BASED SAUCEPAN, brown the rosemary, garlic, bay leaf and the floured rabbit joints in oil.

Add the artichoke hearts cut in half and sprinkle with salt and hot red pepper.

Cover with the stock (from a bouillon cube if you like) and cook over medium heat for about an hour, turning over the meat alone but not the artichokes, which could fall apart.

Before turning off the heat, dust with chopped parsley.

In some internal areas of Sicily, this was served up as the main dish at Easter.

COSCIA DI CAPRETTO AL FORNO
ROAST GIGOT OF KID

- GIGOT (LEG) OF KID (FOR A TOTAL OF ABOUT 2 KG / 4 LBS)
- 200 G / 8 OZ SPICY PROVOLA CHEESE
- SPRING ONIONS (SCALLIONS)
- 375 ML / 12 FL OZ / 1½ CUPS DRY WHITE WINE
- 50 G / 2 OZ / ½ CUP GRATED CACIOCAVALLO OR ANOTHER STRONG-FLAVOURED CHEESE
- 1 TBSP DRY BREADCRUMBS
- OLIVE OIL
- SALT AND PEPPER

PREPARATION TIME: 2 HOURS

F LATTEN OUT the kid gigots with a meat pounder. Make a few small slits in the meat and insert pieces of provola, slices of spring onion, salt and pepper. Oil and crumb a baking dish, lay the meat in it, douse with the wine and sprinkle over a trickle of oil and the grated caciocavallo cheese. Roast for about 1½ hours in a hot oven.

COSCIOTTO DI AGNELLO RIPIENO
STUFFED LEG OF LAMB

♦

- 1 KG / 2 LBS BONED LEG OF LAMB
- 1 LAMB'S LIVER OR 300 G ¾ LB MINCED (GROUND) MEAT
- 500 G / 1 LB PEAS
- 4 SMALL ONIONS
- 1 MEDIUM-SIZED ONION, CHOPPED
- 150 G / 6 OZ BACON
- 50 G / 2 OZ / ½ CUP GRATED CACIOCAVALLO CHEESE
- 50 G / 2 OZ / ½ CUP DRY BREADCRUMBS
- 2 EGGS
- 125 ML / 4 FL OZ / ½ CUP WHITE WINE
- PARSLEY
- SALT AND PEPPER
- OIL

♦

PREPARATION TIME: 1½ HOURS

SAUTÉ TWO CHOPPED ONIONS in some oil in a saucepan. Add the peas, cover with water, season with salt and pepper and leave to cook over a low flame. In another saucepan, brown the two other onions which have been chopped up with the bacon, and the liver cut into pieces or the minced meat. Add a little water, season with salt and pepper and cook for 15-20 minutes until the sauce has reduced. Leave to cool, add the breadcrumbs, grated cheese, chopped parsley, peas and the beaten eggs. Blend the mixture evenly. Stuff the leg of lamb with it and tie or sew it up so that there is no spillage. Colour the chopped onion in a frying pan, add the stuffed leg and sear it. Pour in a glass of white wine and allow to evaporate. Season with salt and pepper and cover with the lid. Cook for another 45 minutes, adding hot water from time to time. Serve the leg hot, accompanied by the gravy in the pan.

FALSOMAGRO
STUFFED MEAT ROLL

◆

- 500 G / 1 LB SLICE OF BEEF (IN ONE PIECE)
- 300 G / ¾ LB MINCED (GROUND) BEEF
- 50 G / 2 OZ / ½ CUP DRY BREADCRUMBS
- 50 G / 2 OZ / 8 TBSP GRATED CHEESE (PECORINO OR PARMESAN)
- 3 EGGS, 2 OF THEM HARD-BOILED
- 125 ML / 4 FL OZ / ½ CUP DRY WHITE WINE
- 1 ONION
- 60 ML / 2 FL OZ / ¼ CUP MILK
- BASIL
- PARSLEY

◆

PREPARATION TIME: 3 HOURS

MIX THE MINCED MEAT with the cheese, breadcrumbs, milk, an egg, the chopped parsley, salt and pepper. Spread the mixture over the slice of beef, place the hard-boiled eggs lengthways, roll up the meat and tie it. In a saucepan, sauté the sliced onion in oil, add the "falsomagro" and allow to brown. Douse with wine and, when it has evaporated, cover the meat with hot water.

Cook gently until a thick gravy has formed (this makes an excellent sauce for serving with spaghetti).

VARIATION: you can cook the "falsomagro" in a moderate oven for about an hour; when half-cooked, add peeled potatoes in small chunks.

You can cook the meat in home-made tomato sauce and, should you wish to make it richer, add, half-way through, potatoes cut into chunks and/or peas.

You may use a different stuffing: replace the minced meat with an omelette (plain or with onions or aromatic herbs) and a slice of mortadella, all rolled up inside the meat slice.

Another kind of filling could be hard-boiled eggs, finely-sliced spring onions and fresh cheese (primosale or provola or caciocavallo or Tuscan or Sardinian caciottina, etc.).

GIRELLO ALLA PALERMITANA
VEAL PALERMO-STYLE

- 1 KG / 2 LBS TOP ROUND OF VEAL
- 500 G / 1 LB WHITE-SKINNED ONIONS
- ¼ L / ½ PT / 1 CUP DRY WHITE WINE
- 250 ML / 8 FL OZ / 1 CUP OLIVE OIL
- 1 TBSP TOMATO CONCENTRATE
- BAY LEAF
- ROSEMARY
- SALT AND PEPPER

◆

PREPARATION TIME: 2 HOURS

SLICE THE ONIONS very finely and colour in half the olive oil over very low heat until well-cooked.

Sear the meat with the herbs and the remaining oil in a meat tin (baking pan). Add the cooked onions to the meat and pour on the wine. Season with salt and pepper.

Cook in a hot oven for about 90 minutes.

When the meat is ready, purée the onion gravy in a "mouli légumes" (food mill) and add the tomato concentrate to it.

Carve the meat thinly and serve masked in the onion sauce.

You could serve some of the cream of onions on macaroni noodles or spaghetti.

GIRELLO IMBOTTITO
STUFFED TOP ROUND OF VEAL

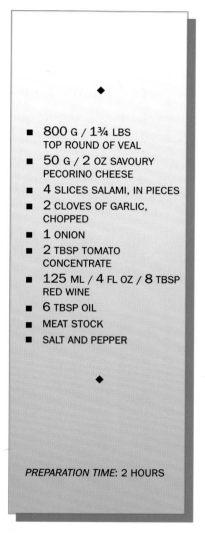

◆

- 800 G / 1¾ LBS TOP ROUND OF VEAL
- 50 G / 2 OZ SAVOURY PECORINO CHEESE
- 4 SLICES SALAMI, IN PIECES
- 2 CLOVES OF GARLIC, CHOPPED
- 1 ONION
- 2 TBSP TOMATO CONCENTRATE
- 125 ML / 4 FL OZ / 8 TBSP RED WINE
- 6 TBSP OIL
- MEAT STOCK
- SALT AND PEPPER

◆

PREPARATION TIME: 2 HOURS

MAKE A FEW SLITS in the piece of meat and fill up with cheese, garlic and salami. Season with salt and pepper. Tie the meat up well to keep the filling in. Sear the meat in a saucepan with the finely-sliced onion, turning frequently until brown all over.

Dissolve the tomato concentrate in the glass of red wine and douse the meat with it. When the wine has evaporated, add the meat stock a little at a time and cook over moderate heat for about an hour. Beware of the meat sticking to the pan.

INVOLTINI DI CARNE
VEAL ROULADES

- 600 G / 1½ LB VEAL IN 8 THIN SLICES
- 2 ONIONS
- 30 G / 1 OZ / 4 TBSP PINE-NUTS
- 30 G / 1 OZ / 3 TBSP SULTANAS OR RAISINS
- 50 G / 2 OZ SALAMI
- 4 TBSP DRY BREADCRUMBS
- 2 TBSP GRATED CACIOCAVALLO OR PARMESAN CHEESE
- 60 ML / 2 FL OZ / ¼ CUP HOME-MADE TOMATO SAUCE
- 10 BAY LEAVES
- SALT AND PEPPER
- OLIVE OIL

PREPARATION TIME: 2 HOURS

CHOP AN ONION FINELY and cook in a little water and oil. When cooked, add the breadcrumbs and a trickle of oil and allow to blend over the heat for a few minutes.

When the mixture has cooled down, add the cheese, the pine-nuts, the sultanas, the roughly-chopped salami, salt and pepper. Moisten the mixture with the tomato sauce.

Cut the slices of meat into rectangles measuring 1½ x 2½ in. Put a spoonful of the mixture on each slice and roll them up to make roulades. Put them into an oiled baking dish previously lined with breadcrumbs, placing a little onion and a bay leaf between each one. Trickle some oil over and bake in a hot oven for 15 minutes.

POLPETTE AL LIMONE
LEMON-FLAVOURED PATTIES

- 500 G / 1 LB MINCED (GROUND) MEAT
- 100 G / 4 OZ / ⅔ CUP WHITE FLOUR
- 80 G / 3 OZ / ⅔ CUP GRATED PECORINO OR PARMESAN CHEESE
- 80 G / 3 OZ / ¾ CUP DRY BREADCRUMBS
- SPRIG OF PARSLEY
- 125 ML / 4 FL OZ / ½ CUP OF MILK
- 1 LEMON
- BASIL, SALT AND PEPPER
- OIL

PREPARATION TIME: 20 MINUTES

PUT THE MEAT, grated cheese, breadcrumbs, chopped basil, salt and pepper in a bowl.

Blend well with the milk and form little squashed, olive-shaped balls. Roll in the flour and brown in a little oil in a frying pan, turning them over. Pour on enough hot water just to cover. Cook over moderate heat until the excess liquid has evaporated and the sauce is nice and thick. Before turning off the heat, dust with parsley and pour over the lemon juice. This dish used to be served in my family when there was someone who could not eat eggs.

POLPETTE AL SUGO
CROQUETTES WITH TOMATO SAUCE

♦

- 500 G / 1 LB MINCED (GROUND) MEAT
- 1 KG / 2 LBS TOMATOES
- 80 G / 3 OZ / 12 TBSP GRATED CHEESE
- 50 G / 2 OZ / ½ CUP DRY BREADCRUMBS
- 50 G / 2 OZ CHOPPED MORTADELLA OR SKINLESS SAUSAGE
- 1 EGG
- 1 ONION
- 60 ML / 2 FL OZ / ¼ CUP MILK
- CHOPPED BASIL
- CHOPPED PARSLEY
- SALT AND PEPPER
- OIL

♦

PREPARATION TIME: 45 MINUTES

MAKE THE SAUCE with the roughly-chopped tomatoes, the onion, basil and salt. Cook for 30 minutes and put through a vegetable mill. Meanwhile, in a bowl, mix the minced meat with the mortadella or sausage, the breadcrumbs, the grated cheese, the egg, salt and pepper, and aromatise with parsley and basil. Blend and, if necessary, add a little milk to make the mixture soft. Form little balls, which you will brown in some hot oil in a frying pan.

Transfer to the sauce and cook for 10 minutes.

VARIATION: "polpette" are the basis of Sicilian cuisine; each family has a secret recipe for making them. To the mixture described above, you may add garlic, onion, etc.... They may also be cooked in the sauce without browning them in oil beforehand. In this way, they are easier on the digestion.

POLPETTE ALL'AGRODOLCE

PATTIES IN A SWEET AND SOUR SAUCE

◆

- 700 G / 1½ LB MINCED (GROUND) VEAL
- 2 ONIONS
- 2 EGGS
- 100 G / 4 OZ / 1 CUP GRATED PARMESAN CHEESE
- 3 TBSP DRY BREADCRUMBS
- 30 ML / 4 TBSP MILK
- BUNCH OF PARSLEY
- 1 CLOVE OF GARLIC
- 1 BAY LEAF
- 100 G / 4 OZ / 1 CUP ALMONDS, PEELED AND TOASTED
- 60 ML / 2 FL OZ / ¼ CUP WHITE VINEGAR
- 2 TBSP SUGAR
- WHITE FLOUR
- SALT AND PEPPER
- HOT RED PEPPER (OPTIONAL)
- OIL

◆

PREPARATION TIME: 45 MINUTES

IN A BOWL, mix the minced meat with the eggs, the breadcrumbs softened in the milk, the grated Parmesan, the chopped garlic and parsley, salt and pepper. Blend the mixture thoroughly. Roll into little balls, flour and fry them. Prepare the sweet and sour sauce by cooking the sliced onions with oil, salt and hot red pepper for 10 minutes. Then add the vinegar, sugar and bay leaf. Continue cooking until the vinegar has completely evaporated.

Put the little drained balls into a large salad bowl, douse with the sweet and sour sauce straight off the heat and scatter the chopped almonds over.

This dish should be served just warm at room temperature.

POLPETTE DI PANE
CROQUETTES OF BREAD

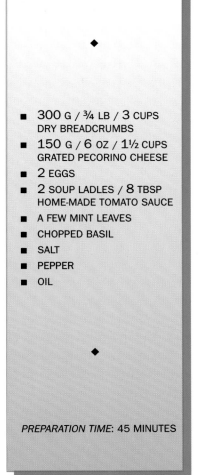

- 300 G / ¾ LB / 3 CUPS DRY BREADCRUMBS
- 150 G / 6 OZ / 1½ CUPS GRATED PECORINO CHEESE
- 2 EGGS
- 2 SOUP LADLES / 8 TBSP HOME-MADE TOMATO SAUCE
- A FEW MINT LEAVES
- CHOPPED BASIL
- SALT
- PEPPER
- OIL

PREPARATION TIME: 45 MINUTES

MIX THE BREADCRUMBS with a whole egg, a yolk and the grated cheese. Season with salt, pepper and the chopped mint and basil. Make little croquettes, which you will dip into the egg white, whisked up with a fork. Dip into the breadcrumbs and fry in hot oil.

Place the croquettes in a saucepan, cover with the tomato sauce and cook for 10 minutes over gentle heat.

POLPETTINE

MEAT BALLS

- 500 G / 1 LB MINCED (GROUND) MEAT
- 500 G / 1 LB ONIONS
- 100 G / 4 OZ / 1⅔ CUPS WHITE FLOUR
- 80 G / 3 OZ / 12 TBSP GRATED PECORINO OR PARMESAN CHEESE
- 50 G / 2 OZ / ½ CUP DRY BREADCRUMBS
- 1 EGG
- 1 BOILED POTATO
- SPRIG OF PARSLEY
- 60 ML / 2 FL OZ / ¼ CUP MILK
- BASIL
- SALT, PEPPER, AND OIL

PREPARATION TIME: 1 HOUR

PUT THE MEAT, grated cheese, bread, potato (mashed in a ricer) and the egg in a bowl. Season with salt and pepper and aromatise with the basil and parsley. Work the mixture together thoroughly, if necessary adding a little milk to soften it. Form tiny, round balls, which you will place on a large plate with the flour. Sweat the chopped or finely-sliced onion in a little oil in a pan, allowing it to colour without frying. Arrange the floured meat balls on the onion, stir carefully and cover with hot water. Check the salt and pepper and turn off the heat when the sauce is rather dense (excellent for serving on spaghetti).

THIS DISH used to be prepared on special occasions or for convalescents as it was considered easily digestible and very nutritious.

POLPETTONE
MEAT ROLL

♦

- 700 G / 1½ LBS MINCED (GROUND) MEAT
- 200 G / 8 OZ FRESH SAUSAGE MEAT
- 200 G / 8 OZ PRIMOSALE CHEESE
- 100 G / 4 OZ VEGETABLES IN SEASON (GLOBE ARTICHOKES, COURGETTES/ZUCCHINI, SWISS CHARD OR SPINACH)
- 4 WHOLE EGGS
- 3 TBSP GRATED CACIOCAVALLO OR PECORINO OR PARMESAN OR ANOTHER RIPE CHEESE
- 3 TBSP DRY BREADCRUMBS
- 50 G / 2OZ SALAMI
- 125 ML / 4 FL OZ / ½ CUP DRY, WHITE WINE
- BUNCH OF PARSLEY
- 1 CLOVE OF GARLIC
- 30 ML / 2 TBSP MILK
- TWIG OF ROSEMARY
- SALT AND PEPPER
- OIL

♦

PREPARATION TIME: 1½ HOURS

BOIL TWO EGGS until hard and the vegetables, separately. Mix the minced meat with two whole eggs, caciocavallo, breadcrumbs, milk and the chopped parsley and garlic in a bowl. Season with salt and pepper.

Work the mixture at length and, if it is too soft, add some grated cheese. Sprinkle a sheet of greaseproof (wax) paper with flour, spread the meat mixture out to form a rectangle and place the cooked vegetables, the sliced salami and hard-boiled eggs, the crumbled, uncooked sausage meat and the sliced primosale in the centre.

Make a meat roll by wrapping the greaseproof paper round, flour it and lay in a heated, oiled baking tin. Place the twig of rosemary on top.

Bake in a hot oven for 10 minutes. Turn it over, douse with a glass of white wine and continue cooking for another 45 minutes, sprinkling with more wine, if necessary.

POLLO ALL'ARANCIA
ORANGE-FLAVOURED CHICKEN

- 1 WHOLE CHICKEN
- 2 TBSP ORANGE MARMALADE
- JUICE OF 5 ORANGES
- BAY LEAF
- ROSEMARY
- SALT AND PEPPER

PREPARATION TIME: 1 HOUR

CLEAN THE CHICKEN WELL, dry it and spread the orange marmalade all round the body cavity. Brown in oil, along with the bay leaf and the rosemary.
When nicely coloured, pour in the orange juice to cover. Season with salt and pepper. Roast in a hot oven for an hour. Serve garnished with slices of orange.

POLLO AL VINO ROSSO
CHICKEN IN RED WINE

- 1 CHICKEN
- 1 L / 2 PTS / 4 CUPS RED WINE
- ROSEMARY
- SAGE
- SALT AND PEPPER

PREPARATION TIME: 2 HOURS

JOINT THE CHICKEN, rinse and dry it well. Arrange the chicken pieces in an oiled casserole. Season with the herbs, salt and pepper. Douse with red wine and bake in a moderate oven for about an hour.

VARIATION: you may add a handful of dried mushrooms, refreshed in hot water, or else 200 g (8 oz / 2 cups) fresh mushrooms.

POLLO RIPIENO
STUFFED CHICKEN

◆

- 1 BONED CHICKEN
- 300 G / ¾ LB MINCED (GROUND) BEEF
- 150 G / 6 OZ CHICKEN LIVERS
- 100 G / 4 OZ / 1 CUP GRATED PECORINO OR PARMESAN CHEESE
- 50 G / 2 OZ / ½ CUP DRY BREADCRUMBS
- 2 EGGS
- 125-250 ML / ½ TO 1 CUP WHITE WINE
- BASIL
- PARSLEY
- SALT AND PEPPER
- OIL

◆

PREPARATION TIME: 45 MINUTES

CHOP UP THE LIVERS AND SAUTÉ. In a bowl, place the minced beef, eggs, cheese, breadcrumbs, livers and the chopped basil and parsley. Season with salt and pepper, mix well and use to stuff the body cavity of the chicken. Sew up the opening so that the stuffing does not spill out.

Sear the chicken all over in oil in a meat tin (baking pan), pour on the wine and allow to evaporate. Transfer the tin to a moderate oven for 1½ hours.

Pour on some wine and hot water from time to time to keep the meat tender. Serve with roast potatoes.

VARIATION: the stuffed chicken may be cooked in stock: cover with water and throw in some parsley stalks, onion, a potato and a stick of celery. In this case, the accompaniments will be the same as for boiled meats.

SALSICCIA AL FORNO CON PATATE

BAKED SAUSAGES AND POTATOES

- 500 G / 1 LB SAUSAGES
- 500 G / 1 LB POTATOES
- 125 ML / 4 FL OZ / 8 TBSP RED WINE

PREPARATION TIME: 1 HOUR

PRICK OVER THE SAUSAGES so that they do not burst. Put into a roasting tin or dish with a little oil or just with the wine. Cook on the top of the stove until a froth of fat forms. Skim it off with a spoon, pour on some more wine and pop into a moderate oven for 10 minutes.

Turn the sausages over and add the potatoes cut into pieces. Continue cooking for a further 15-20 minutes.

SALSICCIA CON OLIVE NERE

SAUSAGES WITH BLACK OLIVES

- 500 G / 1 LB SAUSAGES
- 200 G / 8 OZ / 1⅓ CUPS OLIVES
- 60 ML / 2 FL OZ / ¼ CUP WHITE WINE
- OIL

PREPARATION TIME: 30 MINUTES

FRY THE SAUSAGES (pricked over with a fork) in a little oil in a frying pan. Toss in the olives and stir so that they absorb the frying oil. Drench with wine, allow to evaporate and turn off the heat. These marry well with boiled cauliflower, dressed with lemon and olive oil.

If you wish to remove the fat from the sausages, boil them in a little hot water before frying them. Then skim and fry.

SCALOPPE AL MARSALA

CUTLETS WITH MARSALA

- ◆

- 5-6 VEAL CUTLETS
- 125 ML / 4 FL OZ / ½ CUP DRY MARSALA
- WHITE FLOUR
- SALT AND PEPPER
- OIL

◆

PREPARATION TIME: 30 MINUTES

FLOUR THE CUTLETS and cook in a frying pan with a little oil. Turn them over and pour in the Marsala. Continue cooking until almost all the wine has evaporated and there is a thick gravy.

This is a speedily-prepared dish which resolves the dilemma of unexpected visitors.

Thin slices of chicken or turkey may also be used.

Spezzatino con patate
STEW WITH POTATOES

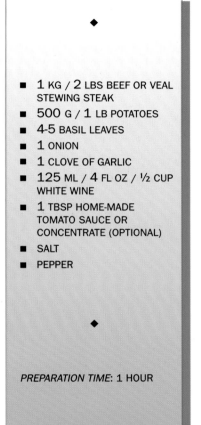

- 1 KG / 2 LBS BEEF OR VEAL STEWING STEAK
- 500 G / 1 LB POTATOES
- 4-5 BASIL LEAVES
- 1 ONION
- 1 CLOVE OF GARLIC
- 125 ML / 4 FL OZ / ½ CUP WHITE WINE
- 1 TBSP HOME-MADE TOMATO SAUCE OR CONCENTRATE (OPTIONAL)
- SALT
- PEPPER

PREPARATION TIME: 1 HOUR

BROWN THE CHOPPED ONION and the whole garlic clove (to be removed once coloured) in some oil in a saucepan. Add the meat and allow the flavours to blend. Pour in the wine and let it evaporate for 5 minutes. Add the potatoes cut into small pieces and cover with hot water. Dress with the basil and tomato (if wished) and season with salt and pepper. Cook over a moderate flame for 30-40 minutes. Add water if necessary.

The sauce is excellent for serving over spaghetti.

VARIATION: Try replacing the potatoes with peas, or with globe artichokes to which you will add a little chopped parsley.

SPIEDINI
SPIT ROAST

◆

- 300 G / ¾ LB MINCED (GROUND) MEAT
- 250 G / ½ LB PRIMOSALE OR MILD PROVOLA
- 250 G / ½ LB SAUSAGES
- 100 G / 4 OZ / 1 CUP DRY BREADCRUMBS
- 50 G / 2 OZ / 8 TBSP GRATED PECORINO OR PARMESAN CHEESE
- 4 SLICES STALE BREAD
- 3 EGGS
- 1 SPRING ONION (SCALLION)
- 60 ML / 2 FL OZ / ¼ CUP MILK
- 60 ML / 2 FL OZ / ¼ CUP RED WINE
- BASIL LEAVES
- SALT AND PEPPER
- OIL FOR FRYING

◆

PREPARATION TIME: 1 HOUR

IN A BOWL, combine the minced meat with the grated cheese, half the breadcrumbs, an egg, the chopped onion, salt and pepper. Form little oval-shaped balls. Cook the sausages cut into little pieces in a little red wine in a frying pan. In the same pan, colour the bread soaked in the milk and cut into small cubes. Thread a piece of bread onto each skewer, followed by a meat ball, a dice of primosale cheese, a piece of sausage and finish up with some bread.

Beat the eggs and a pinch of salt in a bowl and turn the breadcrumbs onto a plate. Coat each skewer first in the egg, then in the breadcrumbs and fry in hot oil.

TRIPPA CON MELANZANE
TRIPE WITH AUBERGINE OR EGGPLANT

◆

- 1 KG / 2 LBS READY-COOKED TRIPE
- 500 G / 1 LB TINNED TOMATOES
- 3 AUBERGINES (EGGPLANTS)
- 4 TBSP GRATED PECORINO OR PARMESAN CHEESE
- 1 CLOVE OF GARLIC
- BASIL
- DRIED HOT RED PEPPER
- SALT
- OLIVE OIL

◆

PREPARATION TIME: 1½ HOURS

PREPARE THE TOMATO SAUCE with the tinned tomatoes and the garlic, hot red pepper, olive oil, salt and basil.

Arrange a layer of the tripe in a baking dish, then a layer of fried aubergine slices and cover with the sauce. Dredge with the grated cheese. Continue layering the ingredients until they have all been used up. Finish off with sauce and cheese. Bake in a hot oven for 30 minutes.

TRIPPA DI UOVA
OMELETTE IN TOMATO SAUCE

- 6 EGGS
- 500 G / 1 LB RIPE TOMATOES
- 100 G / 4 OZ / 1 CUP GRATED CHEESE
- 1 CLOVE OF GARLIC
- BASIL
- SALT AND PEPPER
- OLIVE OIL

PREPARATION TIME: 45 MINUTES

BEAT THE EGGS in a bowl, season with ⅔ of the grated cheese, salt and pepper. Pour half the eggs into a little oil in a frying pan and make an omelette. Remove from the pan and make a second one with the remaining eggs.

Cut the omelettes into strips. Meanwhile, sauté the whole garlic clove in a little oil in a pan, preferably an earthenware one. Add the skinned, seeded, roughly-chopped tomatoes, season with salt and pepper and add the chopped basil. Cook for 5 minutes, stirring well. Toss in the omelette strips and continue cooking for another 5 minutes. Arrange on a serving dish and dust with grated cheese.

FISH

"Carni metti carni,
pisci ti nutrisci.."
(Meat makes you stalwart, fish nurtures you)

F. Consolo "La gastronomia nei proverbi" Novedit Milano

Surrounded by three seas, Sicily has a great variety and quantity of fish ranging from bluefish to lobsters and shrimps of various sizes, right up to the swordfish, a sovereign fish.

There are humbler fish and more prized ones in sufficient quantity just to make sure that Sicilians do not suffer from hunger.

The recipes presented here are for fish which can be found fresh in most markets and also frozen nowadays. They are some time-honoured, tasty and nourishing recipes such as the "sarde a beccafico" or the tuna in a vinegar and onion sauce which used to be considered poor man's meals but which now find room on the menus of the best restaurants.

In the same way, the Benedictine nuns' "tortino di alici" used to be served as an appetiser in the baronial cuisine. I, however, have written it up as a main dish, because I find that it is complete when it follows a first course of pasta with seafood.

ALICI ALL'AGRODOLCE

FRESH ANCHOVIES IN A SWEET AND SOUR SAUCE

- 1 KG / 2 LBS FRESH ANCHOVIES, SCALED AND GUTTED
- 150 G / 6 OZ / 1 CUP WHITE FLOUR
- 60 ML / 2 FL OZ / ¼ CUP VINEGAR
- CLOVE OF GARLIC
- 25 G / 1 OZ / 2 TBSP GRANULATED SUGAR
- BAY LEAF
- FRESH MINT
- SALT AND PEPPER

PREPARATION TIME: 1 HOUR

COAT THE FISH with flour and fry. Sauté the garlic and bay leaf in a little oil in a pan. Add the vinegar with the sugar and cook for one or two minutes.

Draw off the heat and pour over the fried fish. Garnish with fresh mint.

VARIATION: fry the fish. In the same oil, put two crushed cloves of garlic with two or three tablespoons of water, a pinch of oregano and 4 tablespoons of vinegar. Boil for 10 minutes, then pour over the fish.

I recommend preparing this recipe a few days before serving it at the table.

ALICI DEL CONVENTO DELLE BENEDETTINE

GRATIN OF FRESH ANCHOVIES

- 1 KG / 2 LBS FRESH ANCHOVIES, SCALED AND GUTTED
- 100 G / 4 OZ / ⅔ CUP GREEN OLIVES
- 50 G / 2 OZ / ½ CUP DRY BREADCRUMBS
- 30 G / 1 OZ / 1 TBSP PINE-NUTS
- 30 G / 1 OZ / 2 TBSP CAPERS
- 3 ORANGES
- 2 LEMONS
- BUNCH OF PARSLEY

PREPARATION TIME: 1½ HOURS

ARRANGE THE SLICED, peeled lemon over the bottom of a baking dish and place the anchovies on top. Sprinkle with the olives, pine-nuts, parsley and capers, all chopped up together. Make another layer of lemons, anchovies and the chopped mixture. Top the final layer with the breadcrumbs, fried in a little oil. Bake in a hot oven for 30 minutes, add the orange juice and return to the oven for a further half-hour.

Allow me to make a valuable suggestion: when you peel the lemons, be careful to remove the white pith which would otherwise make the dish bitter.

ALICI IN POLPETTA

FRESH ANCHOVY FISHCAKES

◆

- 1 KG / 2 LBS FRESH ANCHOVIES OR SARDINES
- 3 MEDIUM-SIZED BOILED POTATOES
- 3 TBSP GRATED CACIOCAVALLO OR PARMESAN CHEESE
- 25 G / 1 OZ / 2½ TBSP RAISINS
- 25 G / 1 OZ / 2½ TBSP PINE-NUTS
- 2 LEMONS
- BUNCH OF PARSLEY
- 1 EGG
- 1 TBSP DRY BREADCRUMBS
- CLOVE OF GARLIC, CHOPPED
- FLOUR
- SALT AND PEPPER
- OIL FOR FRYING

◆

PREPARATION TIME: 1 HOUR

GUT AND SCALE THE FISH, rinse, drain well and chop up with a knife. Mix the fish with the egg, breadcrumbs, cheese, raisins and pine-nuts in a bowl. Add the chopped garlic and parsley and the mashed potatoes. Season with salt and pepper. Make small fishcakes, coat with flour and deep fry in oil. Serve hot with the lemon juice.

PICKLES were generally served with this dish (a mixture of vegetables: carrots, cauliflower, celery, etc., first blanched in water and vinegar and then preserved in oil or vinegar).

BACCALÀ AL FORNO
BAKED SALT COD

◆

- ■ 1 KG / 2 LB SALT COD, PREVIOUSLY SOAKED
- ■ 500 G / 1 LB BOILED POTATOES
- ■ 2 ONIONS
- ■ 2 CLOVES OF GARLIC
- ■ 3 CLOVES
- ■ BUNCH OF PARSLEY,
- ■ CHOPPED
- ■ SALT AND PEPPER
- ■ OLIVE OIL

◆

PREPARATION TIME: 1½ HOURS

S LICE THE ONION FINELY. Boil the salt cod for 10 minutes, drain and leave to cool. Remove the skin and bones. Oil a baking tin or dish and arrange a layer of sliced potato in the bottom. Put half the salt cod fillets on top of the potatoes and scatter half the sliced onions over. Repeat the layers of potatoes, fish and onions. Season with pepper and the parsley, garlic and cloves, all chopped up. Sprinkle with oil and bake in a hot oven for an hour.

BACCALÀ IN INSALATA
SALT COD SALAD

◆

- ■ 1 KG / 2 LB SALT COD, PREVIOUSLY SOAKED
- ■ 2 LEMONS
- ■ SPRIG OF PARSLEY
- ■ OLIVE OIL

◆

PREPARATION TIME: 1 HOUR

R INSE THE SALT COD and place in a pan with the parsley and a few drops of vinegar. Cook for 15 minutes. Drain and allow to cool. Skin and bone the fish. Season with olive oil, lemon juice and chopped parsley.

VARIATION: chop up an onion and a clove of garlic and brown in a little oil in a pan. Add two or three ripe tomatoes cut into pieces. Cook for about 10 minutes and throw in 100 g (4 oz / ⅔ cup) pitted black olives.
Add the "baccalà", stir and scatter the chopped parsley over before drawing off the heat.

BACCALÀ IN SFINCIONE
SALT COD BAKED IN TOMATO SAUCE

◆

- 1 KG / 2 LB SALT COD, PREVIOUSLY SOAKED
- 1 KG / 2 LB RIPE TOMATOES
- 200 G / 8 OZ / 1⅓ CUPS BLACK OLIVES, PITTED (STONED)
- 100 G / 4 OZ / 1 CUP DRY BREADCRUMBS
- 2 LARGE ONIONS
- SPRIG OF PARSLEY
- 60ML / 4 TBSP VINEGAR

◆

PREPARATION TIME: 1½ HOURS

R INSE THE SALT COD and boil in water to which you have added a sprig of parsley and the vinegar. Drain and leave to cool. Skin and bone the fish and place in an oiled baking tin or ovenproof dish. Slice the onion finely and sauté in a pan with a little oil. Add the skinned, seeded and roughly-chopped tomatoes. Season with salt and pepper and cook for about 20 minutes until the sauce has thickened. Pour the sauce over the "baccalà", garnish with pieces of olive, sprinkle with breadcrumbs and oil and bake in a moderate oven for 20-30 minutes.

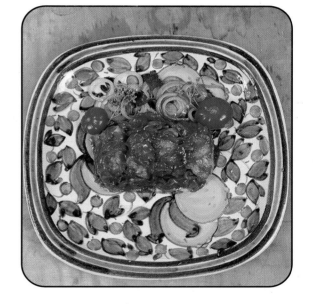

FILETTI DI ORATA CON CREMA DI ZUCCHINE
FILLETS OF GILTHEAD WITH COURGETTE PURÉE

◆

- 12 FILLETS GILTHEAD OR SEA BREAM
- 24 BABY CLAMS
- 500 G / 1 LB COURGETTES (ZUCCHINI)
- 2 CLOVES OF GARLIC
- SPRIG OF PARSLEY
- 60 ML / 4 TBSP WHITE WINE
- 4 TBSP HOME-MADE TOMATO SAUCE
- WHITE FLOUR
- SALT AND PEPPER

◆

PREPARATION TIME: 1 HOUR

C UT THE COUR-GETTES into rings and stew with oil, chopped parsley and garlic, salt, pepper and half a glass of water. As soon as it has all cooled, liquidise briefly. Meanwhile, clean the clams and put them in a pan over gentle heat until the shells open. Coat the fish fillets in flour and fry in a little oil.

Put the courgette purée into a wide baking tin or dish and arrange the gilthead or sea bream fillets and the clams on top. Moisten with the tomato sauce and the white wine and bake for 10 minutes in a hot oven.

PESCE SPADA A COTOLETTA
SWORDFISH CUTLETS

◆

- 4 SWORDFISH STEAKS (ABOUT 300 G / ½ LB EACH)
- 2 EGGS
- 2 LEMONS
- 100 G / 4 OZ / ⅔ CUP WHITE FLOUR
- 100 G / 4 OZ / 1 CUP DRY BREADCRUMBS
- CLOVE OF GARLIC
- PARSLEY
- SALT AND PEPPER

◆

PREPARATION TIME: 30 MINUTES

BEAT THE EGGS WITH A FORK. Take two plates; on one, mix the breadcrumbs with the chopped garlic and parsley, salt and pepper; on the other, put the flour. Heat some oil in a frying pan.

Dip each fish steak into the flour, then into the egg and finally coat with breadcrumbs. Fry in hot oil.

Arrange the cutlets on a serving dish and garnish with lemon wedges and parsley sprigs.

———

THESE CUTLETS are generally served with boiled potatoes cut into small chunks and fried in really hot oil.

PESCE SPADA AL FORNO

BAKED SWORDFISH

◆

- 4 SWORDFISH STEAKS
- 4 LEMONS
- 150 G / 6 OZ / 1½ CUPS DRY BREADCRUMBS
- 1 TSP OREGANO
- HOT RED PEPPER
- OLIVE OIL

◆

PREPARATION TIME: 1½ HOURS

MACERATE THE FISH with the oil, lemon juice, grated zest of 1 lemon, oregano, salt and a pinch of hot red pepper for 30 minutes.

Dip the slices of fish into the breadcrumbs and arrange in an oiled oven dish. Bake for 30 minutes in a hot oven, remembering to turn the slices over half-way through.

Serve garnished with slices of lemon.

———————

THIS IS A RICH MAN'S DISH because the fish must be very fresh and rather small.

Traditionally it is served with potatoes cooked over charcoal, but today jacket potatoes wrapped in aluminium foil and baked in the oven will do fine.

PESCE SPADA AL POMODORO

SWORDFISH IN TOMATO SAUCE

◆

- 4 SWORDFISH STEAKS
- 1 KG / 2 LBS RIPE TOMATOES OR 2½ CUPS TINNED PLUM TOMATOES
- 200 G / 8 OZ / 1⅓ CUPS GREEN OLIVES
- 50 G / 2 OZ / 4 TBSP CAPERS
- 4 ANCHOVY FILLETS
- 60 ML / 4 TBSP DRY WHITE WINE
- PARSLEY
- SALT AND PEPPER
- OLIVE OIL

◆

PREPARATION TIME: 1 HOUR

PUT INTO A PAN: the oil, the skinned, seeded and roughly-chopped tomatoes, the pitted olives cut into pieces, the capers and the anchovy fillets. Blend the flavours over a moderate heat for 5 minutes, add a glass of hot water and continue cooking for 20 minutes until the sauce becomes smooth. Arrange the slices of swordfish over the sauce, spray with white wine and cook a further 15-20 minutes.

Before drawing off the heat, dredge with salt, pepper and chopped parsley.

PESCE SPADA ALLA MESSINESE
SWORDFISH FROM MESSINA

- 4 SWORDFISH STEAKS
- 500 G / 1 LB FRESH TOMATOES OR 2½ CUPS TINNED PLUM TOMATOES
- 500 G / 1 LB BOILED POTATOES
- 200 G / 8 OZ / 1⅓ CUPS OLIVES, PITTED (STONED)
- 50 G / 2 OZ / 4 TBSP CAPERS
- 1 MEDIUM-SIZED ONION
- PARSLEY
- SALT AND PEPPER

PREPARATION TIME: 1 HOUR

SAUTÉ THE CHOPPED ONION in a large pan. Add the roughly-chopped olives and tomatoes (skinned and seeded) and the capers. Cook slowly for 10 minutes. Arrange half of the sliced potatoes in a roomy, oiled baking dish, cover with the swordfish slices and mask with the sauce. Cover it all with the remaining potato. Bake in a moderate oven for about 20 minutes. Take the dish out of the oven, remove the top layer of potato and season the fish with salt, pepper and chopped parsley. Return to the switched-off oven which is still warm. Serve when a moderate temperature has been reached.

PESCE SPADA ALLA GRIGLIA CON SALMORIGLIO
GRILLED SWORDFISH WITH "SALMORIGLIO" SAUCE

◆

- 4 SWORDFISH STEAKS
- 3 LEMONS, SQUEEZED
- HANDFUL OF CHOPPED PARSLEY
- CLOVE OF GARLIC, CUT IN HALF
- PINCH OREGANO
- SALT AND PEPPER
- OLIVE OIL

◆

PREPARATION TIME: 30 MINUTES

GRILL THE SWORDFISH. Make the "salmoriglio" sauce by pouring a little oil into a pan and gradually beating in a glass of hot water with a fork, then add the lemon juice, the garlic (to be removed), the oregano and the parsley. Cook for 5 minutes in a "bain-marie", still beating with the fork. Pour the sauce over the swordfish steaks and serve.

MY FATHER used to say that swordfish was best grilled because you could smell the sea. Cooking it differently would not bring out its freshness and flavour to the full.

PESCE SPADA CON LE CIPOLLE E L'ACETO
SWORDFISH WITH ONION AND VINEGAR

◆

- 4 SWORDFISH STEAKS
- 2-3 TOMATOES
- 2 ONIONS
- 2 STICKS OF CELERY
- 100 G / 4 OZ / ⅔ CUP GREEN OLIVES
- 50 G / 2 OZ / ¼ CUP CAPERS
- 50 G / 2 OZ / ⅓ CUP WHITE FLOUR
- 60 ML / 4 TBSP VINEGAR
- SALT AND PEPPER
- OLIVE OIL

◆

PREPARATION TIME: 1 HOUR

COAT THE FISH steaks in flour and fry. Put the finely-sliced onion, the chopped celery, the capers and the pitted olives cut into pieces in a little oil in a pan. Add the tomatoes, skinned, seeded and roughly-chopped. Blend the flavours for 10 minutes on the top of

the stove, pour in a glass of water and continue cooking until the sauce has reduced. Lay the fried swordfish steaks on the sauce and sprinkle over the vinegar. When it has evaporated, turn off the heat.

PESCE SPADA IN INVOLTINO
SWORDFISH ROLLS

◆

- **12** SWORDFISH STEAKS
- **150** G / **6** OZ / **1½** CUPS DRY BREADCRUMBS, FRIED IN OIL
- **6** FRESH ANCHOVY FILLETS IN OIL
- **2** CHOPPED CLOVES OF GARLIC
- **2** LEMONS
- **1** ONION
- A FEW BAY LEAVES
- SALT
- HOT RED PEPPER

◆

PREPARATION TIME: 1 HOUR

DISSOLVE THE FRESH ANCHOVY fillets in their oil over low heat. Add the breadcrumbs, the chopped garlic, the salt and hot red pepper. Spread the filling over the fish steaks and roll them up tightly. Thread them onto a skewer, alternating them with a piece of onion and a bay leaf. Sprinkle oil and lemon juice over. Bake in a moderate oven for 20 minutes, being careful that nothing dries out. The swordfish must be sliced thinly for this dish.

RUOTA DI PESCE SPADA AL FORNO

BAKED SWORDFISH WHEEL

◆

- 1 KG / 2 LB PIECE OF SWORDFISH (THE CENTRAL PART OF THE FISH)
- 500 G / 1 LB RIPE TOMATOES
- 4 CLOVES OF GARLIC
- OREGANO
- BASIL
- SALT
- PEPPERCORNS
- OLIVE OIL

◆

PREPARATION TIME: 2 HOURS

QUARTER THE GARLIC CLOVES. Stud the fish with the garlic and the pepper corns. Cover the base of a baking dish with some of the tomatoes, skinned, seeded and roughly-chopped. Season with salt and arrange the fish on top. Cover with the remaining pieces of tomato, season with oregano, basil, salt and oil. Bake in a moderate oven for an hour and a half. Serve with potatoes grilled over charcoal or oven-baked in aluminium foil.

PESCE STOCCO ALLA GHIOTTA
SMOTHERED STOCKFISH

♦

- 1 KG / 2 LBS STOCKFISH, PREVIOUSLY SOAKED
- 4 SPRING ONIONS (SCALLIONS) OR SMALL ONIONS
- 100 G / 4 OZ / ½ CUP PICKLED CAPERS
- 100 G / 4 OZ / ⅔ CUP PITTED (STONED) BLACK OLIVES
- SMALL HEAD OF CELERY
- 500 G / 1 LB TIN (CAN) PLUM TOMATOES (2½ CUPS)
- 500 G / 1 LB POTATOES
- 125 ML / 8 TBSP DRY WHITE WINE
- WHITE FLOUR
- HOT RED PEPPER
- OIL

♦

PREPARATION TIME: 1½ HOUR

IN A DEEP FRYING PAN, sauté the spring onions cut into strips with the floured pieces of fish. Add the capers, the celery cut into rings, the potatoes in small chunks and the olives. Moisten with a glass of white wine which you will allow to evaporate. Add the tomatoes and cook slowly for about an hour.

If necessary, pour on a little water during the cooking, so that the sauce is not so thick.

POLIPETTI IN TEGAME

STEWED MOSCARDINI

- ◆
- 1 KG / 2 LBS MOSCARDINI OR SQUID
- 400 G / 14 OZ / 2 CUPS TINNED TOMATOES
- 1 SMALL ONION
- CLOVE OF GARLIC
- BUNCH OF PARSLEY
- 60 ML / 2 FL OZ / ¼ CUP WHITE WINE
- WHITE FLOUR
- SALT
- HOT RED PEPPER
- ◆

PREPARATION TIME: 1 HOUR

CLEAN THE "MOSCARDINI" and leave to drain. Coat with flour. Sauté the chopped onion and garlic in a pan. Add the "moscardini" and brown well, then douse with the white wine. When it has completely evaporated, add the skinned tomatoes. Continue cooking for 30 minutes over gentle heat.

Sprinkle with chopped parsley before drawing off the heat.

RONDELLE DI PALOMBO

PALOMBO IN TOMATO SAUCE

- ◆
- 12 PALOMBO FISH FILLETS
- 2 CLOVES OF GARLIC
- 500 G / 1 LB / 2½ CUPS TINNED TOMATOES
- 3 EGGS
- SPRIG OF PARSLEY
- 1 KG / 2 LBS / 8 CUPS DRY BREADCRUMBS
- WHITE FLOUR
- SALT AND PEPPER
- HOT RED PEPPER
- ◆

PREPARATION TIME: 30 MINUTES

RUB SOME SALT and pepper into the fish fillets, coat with flour and steep in the beaten egg for a few hours.

Meanwhile, chop up the garlic and parsley, add the tomatoes and cook the sauce for 15 minutes.

Add salt and hot red pepper. Dip the fish into the breadcrumbs and fry.

Add the fried fish fillets to the sauce and cook for 10 more minutes.

SARDE A BECCAFICO
STUFFED SARDINES

- 1 KG / 2 LBS FRESH SARDINES (IN AN EVEN NUMBER)
- 100 G / 4 OZ / 1 CUP DRY BREADCRUMBS
- 10 ALMONDS, TOASTED AND CHOPPED
- 10 BAY LEAVES
- 8 PITTED (STONED) BLACK OLIVES
- 6 ANCHOVY FILLETS, TINNED OR FRESH
- ZEST OF 2 LEMONS
- 2 TSP GRANULATED SUGAR
- HANDFUL OF PARSLEY
- 1 TBSP PICKLED CAPERS
- 1 TBSP EACH SULTANAS AND PINE-NUTS
- 60 ML / 4 TBSP LEMON JUICE

PREPARATION TIME: 1 HOUR

GUT THE SARDINES, pull off the head and backbone and open up flat. Rinse and dry. Dissolve the anchovies in heated oil, add the breadcrumbs and stir. When cold, add the grated lemon zest, 2 tablespoons sugared lemon juice, the chopped parsley, the capers, sultanas, pine-nuts, olives, almonds, salt and pepper. Stir and add a little olive oil if too dry. Spread the mixture over half the sardines, arrange in an oiled-and-crumbed baking dish and top with the remaining sardines.

Sprinkle with the rest of the lemon juice, place a bay leaf between each fish, trickle over a little olive oil and bake in a hot oven for 15 minutes.

THIS DISH gets its name from a bird very partial to figs which gets plumper and plumper the more it eats. Likewise, this fish "parcel" encourages the most uncontrolled voracity.

SEPPIE IN TEGAME
SMOTHERED CUTTLEFISH

◆

- 1 KG / 2 LBS CUTTLEFISH
- 50 G / 2 OZ / ¼ CUP TOMATO CONCENTRATE
- 1 ONION
- CLOVE OF GARLIC
- 125 ML / 8 TBSP WHITE WINE
- SPRIG OF PARSLEY

◆

PREPARATION TIME: 2 HOURS

GUT AND CLEAN the cuttlefish, removing the sacs of black ink, and cut into rings. Sauté the chopped onion and garlic in some oil in a pan. Add the cuttlefish, salt and pepper. Stir well and pour in the tomato

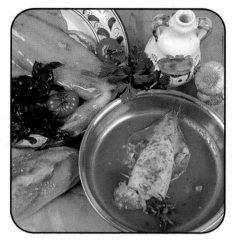

concentrate diluted in the wine. Cook for 20 minutes over a moderate heat.

Sgombri Arrostiti

GRILLED MACKEREL

- **4 MACKEREL**
- **250 ML / 8 FL OZ / 1 CUP VINEGAR**
- **2 LEMONS**
- **PINCH OF OREGANO**
- **SALT**
- **PEPPER**

PREPARATION TIME: 1 HOUR

GUT, BONE AND CLEAN THE MACKEREL, opening them out flat. Marinate in a vinegar-filled bowl for 20 minutes. Drain and grill. Make the "salmoriglio" sauce to baste the fish by chopping up the oregano, salt and pepper with some oil and the lemon juice.

VARIATION: Clean the mackerel, leaving them whole. Make short slits along the body and insert pieces of garlic. Leave the mackerel to steep in a bowl with lemon juice salt, garlic and chopped parsley and to absorb the flavours. Grill (Broil) them, brushing the marinade over with a sprig of rosemary.

SGOMBRI IN COTOLETTA
MACKEREL CUTLETS

- 6 MEDIUM-SIZED MACKEREL
- 3 EGGS
- 200 G / 8 OZ / 2 CUPS DRY BREADCRUMBS
- 1 TBSP GRANULATED SUGAR
- 125 ML / 8 TBSP WHITE WINE VINEGAR
- WHITE FLOUR
- SALT
- HOT RED PEPPER

PREPARATION TIME: 1 HOUR

GUT, BONE, CLEAN AND DRY THE MACKEREL, opening them out flat. Arrange in a bowl and cover with vinegar, salt and hot red pepper. Leave to marinate an hour. Drain the fish, coat with flour, then dip in the beaten egg and finally in the breadcrumbs. Deep fry in olive oil and serve hot.

THIS IS THE FISHERMAN'S Sunday dinner. Blue fish, tuna and sea food used to be poor man's meat. Cutlets were a noble dish and, together with a side-plate of fried potatoes, were a meal fit for a king. A scrumptious dish served after pasta in a seafood sauce.

TONNO CON LE CIPOLLE E L'ACETO
TUNA IN A VINEGAR AND ONION SAUCE

- 4 FRESH TUNA FISH SLICES
- 2-3 TOMATOES
- 2 ONIONS
- 100 G / 4 OZ / ⅔ CUP GREEN OLIVES
- 50 G / 2 OZ / ¼ CUP CAPERS
- 50 G / 2 OZ / ¼ CUP WHITE FLOUR
- 1 STICK OF CELERY
- 60 ML / 4 TBSP VINEGAR
- SALT AND PEPPER
- OLIVE OIL

PREPARATION TIME: 1 HOUR

COAT THE TUNA SLICES in flour and fry. Sauté the thinly-sliced onion in a little oil in a saucepan, add the chopped celery, the capers and the pitted olives cut into pieces. After 5 minutes, add the skinned, seeded and roughly-chopped tomatoes with a glass of hot water.
Cook until the sauce has reduced. Lay the tuna slices on top, spray with vinegar and, when it has evaporated, draw off the heat.

THIS RECIPE used to be prepared when the tuna catch was particularly copious.
The dish keeps for several days and is very good eaten cold. In this case, there must be plenty of "stemperata", the vinegar and onion sauce.

163

TONNO FRESCO AL RAGÙ
FRESH TUNA WITH TOMATO AND PEA SAUCE

◆

- 1 SLICE FRESH TUNA FISH (ABOUT 1 KG / 2 LBS)
- 500 G / 1LB / 2½ CUPS TINNED (CANNED) PLUM TOMATOES
- 250 G / ½LB PEAS
- 6 MINT LEAVES
- 2 CLOVES OF GARLIC, CHOPPED
- WHITE FLOUR
- SALT
- HOT RED PEPPER

◆

PREPARATION TIME: 2 HOURS

RINSE THE TUNA under running water for ten minutes, drain and make slits in the surface into which you will insert the mint leaves, the garlic, the salt and hot red pepper. Coat the tuna slices with flour and fry in a frying pan until golden all over.

Make the tomato sauce separately, adding the peas and leaving to cook for 15 minutes. Pour onto the tuna, with the addition of a glass of water to soften it.

Cook over a slow flame for about an hour. If necessary, add more water.

THIS SAUCE is excellent for serving with bucatini or spaghetti, but then you should increase the quantity of peas and tomatoes.

TOTANI RIPIENI
STUFFED SQUID

◆

- LARGE SQUID
- CLOVES OF GARLIC
- LEMONS
- HARD-BOILED EGG
- 100 G / 4OZ / 1 CUP DRY BREADCRUMBS
- 25 G / 1OZ / 1-2 TBSP GRATED PECORINO OR PARMESAN CHEESE
- SALT
- PEPPER
- OLIVE OIL

◆

PREPARATION TIME: 1½ HOURS

CLEAN THE SQUID, leaving the inksacs intact. Prepare the filling by crumbling the hard-boiled egg in a bowl, adding the breadcrumbs, the chopped garlic and parsley, and seasoning with salt and pepper.

Combine everything with the oil and squeezed lemon juice. Stuff the squid, sew them up and fry for at least thirty minutes. Serve hot with lemon juice.

VARIATION: brown 300 g (¾ lb) baby squid with a clove of garlic, add 50 g (2 oz / ⅓ cup) large black olives, 250 g (½ lb / 1½ cups) sultanas, 25 g (1 oz / 2 tbsp) pine-nuts and the roughly-chopped tomato. Season with salt and pepper and cook for 30 minutes. Before turning off the heat, add a sprig or two of chopped parsley.

DESSERTS AND CONFECTIONERY

"Così amari, tènili cari
così duci, tènili 'nchiusi"
(Look after sour things carefully,
keep sweet things locked up)

E. Alaimo "Proverbi Siciliani" Edit. Martello

When you go into a Sicilian pastry shop, you are met with such a variety of fragrance, colour and choice of sweetmeats that deciding what to eat or buy is difficult. The basic ingredients of these desserts are honey, ricotta cheese, almonds, pistachios and lots of imagination.

They used to be made in the home as pastry shops were very few and many were attached to convents where the nuns made very refined sweet dishes to order.

When sweetmeats were made at home, the women started preparing them several weeks ahead of the religious or secular festivals and, while they worked, their grandmothers or elderly aunts (who directed and supervised the proceedings) would keep the children occupied by getting them to recite prayers or sing sacred hymns. So it is that the names of many sweet dishes are linked to the event or saint that was being celebrated. Two very distinct sweet dishes are associated with Easter: marzipan "sheep" and cassata. Even abroad, these have become the symbol of Sicilian desserts on account of the elegant way in which they are presented as well as for their delectability. It was the Arabs who, around 1200, taught the convent nuns the art of making marzipan and cassata. The story goes that, on the occasion of the Diocesan Synod at Mazara del Vallo, the nuns were forbidden to produce these sweets during Holy Week so as not to get distracted from their religious functions. Nowadays, the preparation is considered too complex and laborious, so very few people get round to making them at home. The cassata recipe that I give here is a simple one, without the marzipan decoration which requires skills of "haute cuisine".

Many recipes which belong to the tradition of Sicilian sweetmeats have been lost because they have not stood up to the recent competition of industrial pastry production which, in Sicily, too, has prevailed over home-cooking in the same domain.

BISCOTTI DI MANDORLE

ALMOND BISCUITS (COOKIES)

◆

- 500 G / 1 LB / 5 CUPS CHOPPED ALMONDS
- 500 G / 1 LB / 2½ CUPS GRANULATED SUGAR
- 6 EGG WHITES
- 1 EGG YOLK
- GRATED ZEST OF 1 LEMON
- 125 ML / 4 FL OZ / ½ CUP MILK
- PINCH CINNAMON
- PINCH SALT

◆

PREPARATION TIME: 30 MINUTES

TURN THE ALMONDS, sugar, grated lemon rind, cinnamon, milk and salt into a bowl and stir well. Whisk the egg whites until stiff and fold gently into the milk mixture. Spoon into a pastry bag. Pipe rounds onto a greased baking tray (or else line it with baking paper). Place an almond in the centre of each one and bake in a hot oven for ten minutes. Remove and brush the biscuits with beaten egg yolk. Return to the hot oven for another 10 minutes.

In my family, these biscuits used to be made at the beginning of December and then kept until Christmas.

BISCOTTI PEPATI

SPICY BISCUITS (COOKIES)

♦

- 500 G / 1 LB / 3½ CUPS WHITE FLOUR
- 150 G / 6 OZ / ¾ CUP GRANULATED SUGAR
- 150 G / 6 OZ / 1½ CUPS CHOPPED ALMONDS
- 100 G / 4 OZ / ½ CUP HONEY
- 50 G / 2 OZ / 4 TBSP LARD OR BUTTER
- PINCH BICARBONATE OF SODA (BAKING SODA)
- PINCH NUTMEG
- PINCH CLOVES
- PINCH CINNAMON
- PINCH PEPPER

♦

PREPARATION TIME: 30 MINUTES

WORK THE FLOUR, sugar and almonds with the butter, honey (dissolved in a little warm water), spices and bicarbonate. Roll into thick fingers which you will place on a greased baking try.
Bake in a hot oven for 10-15 minutes until the biscuits turn golden. Remove the tray from the oven, leave to cool a little, then cut the fingers into slices ½ in thick. Return to the oven for 5 minutes, then turn it off and leave the biscuits to cool inside before removing them.

BISCOTTI REGINA

SESAME BISCUITS (COOKIES)

◆

- 300 G / ¾ LB / 2 CUPS WHITE FLOUR
- 200 G / 8 OZ / 1 CUP LARD OR BUTTER
- 100 G / 4 OZ / ½ CUP GRANULATED SUGAR
- 100 G / 4 OZ / 6 TBSP SESAME SEEDS
- 1 EGG
- PINCH SALT

◆

PREPARATION TIME: 30 MINUTES (PLUS AN HOUR'S REST FOR THE DOUGH)

HEAP THE FLOUR, a pinch of salt and the sugar on a pastry board. Work in the egg and lard or soft butter (not melted). Knead gently until the flour is completely absorbed. If necessary, add half a glass of warm water.

Shape into a ball, wrap in a tea cloth and leave to rest in a warm place for about an hour.

Make fat fingers like breadsticks and cut into lengths of about 2-2½ in. Turn the sesame seeds into a bowl, roll the fingers in them and place on a greased baking try. Bake in a hot oven for about 20 minutes.

BISCOTTI TARALLE
ICED BISCUITS (COOKIES)

- 500 G / 1 LB / 3½ CUPS WHITE FLOUR
- 500 G / 1 LB / 3½ CUPS CORNFLOUR (CORNSTARCH)
- 500 G / 1 LB / 2½ CUPS GRANULATED SUGAR
- 200 G / 8 OZ / 1⅔ CUPS ICING (CONFECTIONERS') SUGAR
- 6 EGGS
- 1 TBSP LARD OR BUTTER
- 1 SACHET / ¼ TSP VANILLA POWDER / ½ TSP VANILLA EXTRACT
- 60 ML / 4 TBSP MILK
- 60 ML / 4 TBSP PLAIN OR JASMINE-FLAVOURED WATER

PREPARATION TIME: 40 MINUTES

SEPARATE THE EGG whites from the yolks. Beat the yolks and sugar to a smooth cream with the sugar. Sprinkle in the flour and cornflour and mix well, adding a little milk. Whisk the egg whites into stiff peaks and gently fold into the flour mixture until evenly blended. Either pipe the mixture from a piping bag or spoon it onto a greased baking tray to form fingers or rings and bake in a moderate oven for about 20 minutes.

To make the glacé icing (frosting), dissolve the icing sugar and the vanilla in the water and heat to just under boiling point. Before turning off the oven, brush the biscuits with the icing. Return to the still-warm oven and leave until it cools off.

BISCOTTI SPAGNOLETTE
RICOTTA BISCUITS (COOKIES)

- 250 G / ½ LB / 1¼ CUPS GRANULATED SUGAR
- 250 G / ½ LB / 1¾ CUPS WHITE FLOUR
- GRATED ZEST OF 1 LEMON
- 25 G / 1 OZ / 2 TBSP VANILLA SUGAR
- 300 G / ¾ LB RICOTTA CHEESE
- 3 EGGS
- MILK

PREPARATION TIME : 1 HOUR

CREAM THE YOLKS with 150 g (6 oz / ¾ cup) sugar. When you have a smooth foam, add the flour and the grated lemon zest a little at a time. Crush the ricotta in a bowl with 100 g (4 oz / ½ cup) sugar and work it in with a fork to get a smooth mixture. A little milk may be added to make it creamier. Whisk the egg whites until stiff and add the vanilla sugar. Slowly mix the ricotta into the creamed yolks and fold in the whisked egg whites. When the mixture is well blended, put some into a piping bag and pipe onto an oiled iron or aluminium baking tray in rounds. Repeat, using up all the paste, and bake for 20 minutes in a hot oven.

BUCCELLATO

DOUGH RING

- 300 G / ¾ LB / 2 CUPS WHITE FLOUR
- 150 G / 6 OZ / ¾ CUP LARD OR BUTTER
- 100 G / 4 OZ / ½ CUP GRANULATED SUGAR
- 125 ML / 4 FL OZ / 8 TBSP MARSALA
- 300 G / ¾ LB / 2 CUPS RAISINS
- 300 G / ¾ LB / 2 CUPS FIGS, CUT UP
- 100 G / 4 OZ / 1 CUP TOASTED ALMONDS
- 100 G / 4 OZ / ½ CUP PLAIN (SEMI-SWEET) CHOCOLATE, BROKEN UP
- 50 G / 2 OZ / ½ CUP WALNUTS, SHELLED
- 1 EGG YOLK
- 50 G / 2 OZ / ½ CUP CHOPPED PISTACHIOS
- PINCH OF CINNAMON
- PINCH OF SALT
- 1 LEMON

PREPARATION TIME: 3 HOURS

WORK THE LARD or butter into the sugar and flour on a pastry board, together with half the Marsala and a pinch of salt. When you have obtained a smooth dough, wrap in a tea towel and leave to rest for about two hours.

Prepare the filling by putting into a saucepan the cut-up figs, the toasted almonds (roughly chopped up with the walnuts), the grated lemon zest, the chocolate, the remaining Marsala and a pinch of cinnamon. Simmer over low heat for about 20 minutes, stirring frequently.

With the aid of a rolling pin, roll the dough into a rectangle about ½ in thick. Pour the cooled filling into the centre, roll up the dough and join the ends to make a ring. Pierce the surface with a fork and place on a greased baking tray. Bake in a hot oven for 30 minutes. Remove the tray from the oven.

Beat an egg yolk energetically and, using a pastry brush or a little cotton wool, spread it over the dough ring. Sprinkle with the chopped pistachios and bake a further 5 minutes. Turn off the oven and leave to cool before removing the cake.

CANNOLI
RICOTTA-FILLED SNAPS

◆

- 150 G / 6 OZ / 1 CUP
  WHITE FLOUR
- 15 G / ½ OZ / ½ TBSP
  BITTER COCOA
- 30 G / 1 OZ / 2 TBSP
  LARD OR BUTTER
- 1 EGG
- 25 G / 1 OZ / 2 TBSP
  GRANULATED SUGAR
- 60 ML / 2 FL OZ / ¼ CUP
  RED WINE OR MARSALA
- 12 STEEL TUBES
- OIL

THE FILLING:
- 500 G / 1 LB / 2¾ CUPS
  RICOTTA CHEESE
- 250 G / 8 OZ / 2 CUPS
  ICING (CONFECTIONERS')
  SUGAR
- 100 G / 4 OZ PLAIN
  (SEMI-SWEET) CHOCOLATE,
  DICED
- 80 G / 3 OZ / ⅜ CUP
  CANDIED PUMPKIN
- 50 G / 2 OZ PISTACHIOS,
  CHOPPED
- PINCH CINNAMON
- CANDIED ORANGE PEEL

◆

PREPARATION TIME: 4 HOURS

HEAP THE FLOUR on a pastry board and carefully work in the egg, lard or butter, sugar, the cocoa dissolved in the red wine or Marsala, and a pinch of salt. When you have a smooth dough, leave to rest for about an hour. With a rolling pin, roll it out into a thin sheet and cut into 4 inch squares. Roll each one diagonally around a steel tube. Delicately press the edges together with a dampened finger. Heat plenty of oil in a deep saucepan and, when it is boiling, immerse the dough-covered tubes. Remove the snaps when they have turned golden and allow to cool.

Meanwhile, work the ricotta with the icing sugar and the cinnamon. Mix well with a wooden spoon, adding a few drops of milk. The cream should be smooth and rather thick. Add the diced chocolate and candied pumpkin at this point, then carefully remove the tubes from the "cannoli" and fill them with a teaspoonful of the filling.

Garnish with pieces of candied orange peel which you will stick into the ends. Dredge the biscuit (cooky) part with a little icing sugar.

CARAMELLE DI CARRUBE
CAROB SQUARES

◆

- 200 G / 8 OZ / 1 CUP HONEY
- 200 G / 8 OZ CAROB PODS
- OIL

◆

PREPARATION TIME: 30 MINUTES

BREAK THE CAROB PODS TO EXTRACT THE SEEDS. Heat them very gently with the honey in a small saucepan. Stir from time to time and when the mixture has become syrupy and caramelised, pour onto an oiled marble slab. Spread the caramel out with a spatula to a thickness of ½ inch . Cut into little squares and leave to dry. They will keep in glass jars.

Even street vendors in Sicily used to sell these sweets. Grandmothers would give them to their grandchildren to suck, especially as a remedy against coughs.

A few decades ago, they disappeared off the market and, unfortunately also from the domestic kitchen.

CASSATA CASALINGA

SICILIAN CASSATA

◆

- 500 G / 1 LB
  SPONGE CAKE
- 500 G / 1 LB
  RICOTTA CHEESE
- 300 G / ¾ LB / 2 CUPS
  ICING (CONFECTIONERS')
  SUGAR
- 100 G / 4 OZ PLAIN
  (SEMI-SWEET) CHOCOLATE
- PINCH GROUND CINNAMON
- SACHET / ¼ TSP VANILLA
  POWDER OR ½ TSP EXTRACT
- 50 G / 2 OZ / ½ CUP
  PISTACHIOS
- 60 ML / 2 FL OZ / 4 TBSP
  VERMOUTH
- 50 G / 2 OZ / ¼ CUP
  CANDIED FRUIT

◆

PREPARATION TIME: 2 HOURS

CUT THE SPONGE CAKE into rectangular slices and place half of them side by side on the bottom of a springform baking tin (with removable sides).

Sprinkle with the vermouth. Work the icing sugar and a few drops of milk into the ricotta to get a creamy mixture, add the diced candied fruit and chocolate, the cinnamon, vanilla and pistachios.

Pour the cream onto the sponge slices, cover with another layer of cake, dust with icing sugar and garnish with the candied fruit.

Chill in the refrigerator for a few hours, but do not freeze.

CASSATINE DI CARNEVALE
CASSATA PASTRIES

- ■ 500 G / 1 LB / 3½ CUPS WHITE FLOUR
- ■ 60 ML / 2 FL OZ / 4 TBSP OLIVE OIL
- ■ PINCH OF SALT
- ■ 500 G / 1 LB RICOTTA CHEESE
- ■ 200 G / ½ LB / 1 CUP GRANULATED SUGAR
- ■ 100 G / 4 OZ / ½ CUP PLAIN (SEMI-SWEET) CHOCOLATE
- ■ PINCH GROUND CINNAMON

PREPARATION TIME: 2 HOURS

KNEAD THE FLOUR WITH THE OIL, salt and a little warm water until the dough is even and elastic. Wrap in a tea towel and leave to rest for about an hour. Make the filling by working the sugar and cinnamon into the ricotta. When you have a creamy mixture, add the diced chocolate.

Roll out the pastry into a thin sheet with a rolling pin. Cut out rounds by pressing an upturned teacup down into the pastry. Put a spoonful of the cream in the centre of each one and close it over, lightly pinching the edges together with your dampened fingers.

Arrange the pastries on a greased baking tray and bake for 40 minutes in a moderate oven.

VARIATION: the pastries may be fried in hot oil or lard and dredged with icing (confectioners') sugar while still hot.

PASTA FRITTA CON MIELE
FRIED LOAVES WITH HONEY

- **1** KG / **2** LBS LEAVENED DOUGH
- **1** TBSP HONEY
- PINCH CINNAMON
- **1** TBSP GRANULATED SUGAR
- OLIVE OIL

PREPARATION TIME: 30 MINUTES

K NEAD THE LEAVENED DOUGH with a tablespoon of oil. Make little flat loaves and fry in hot oil. Place the little loaves on a large serving dish and pour over the honey dissolved in 60 ml (4 tbsp) water.

Dredge with sugar and cinnamon and eat while hot.

THIS DISH has almost disappeared because bread is rarely made at home nowadays.

In Italy, bakers will sell leavened dough across the counter, so half your work is done!

PIGNUCCATA

FRIED PASTRY

◆

- 500 G / 1 LB / 3½ CUPS FLOUR
- 5 EGG YOLKS
- 200 G / 8 OZ / 1 CUP HONEY
- 50 G / 2 OZ / ¼ CUP GRANULATED SUGAR
- 60 ML / 2 FL OZ / ¼ CUP WATER OR ORANGE WATER
- GRATED ZEST OF 1 ORANGE OR LEMON
- PINCH SALT
- PINCH CINNAMON
- VEGETABLE OIL OR LARD FOR FRYING
- ICING (CONFECTIONERS') SUGAR

◆

PREPARATION TIME: 1 HOUR

HEAP THE FLOUR UP on a work surface and pour the yolks, a pinch of salt and the sugar into a hollow in the middle. Knead to a soft, even dough.

Form into fingers of the thickness of breadsticks, cut into small lengths and fry in boiling lard or vegetable oil.

In a small pan, dissolve the honey in the plain or flavoured water with the grated lemon or orange zest. Pile the fried pastries into a pyramid or pine cone (this is where the name comes from) on a serving dish. Dust with icing sugar and cinnamon.

In the Messina district, "pignuccata" is typically served covered with cocoa and lemon icing (frosting).

SFINCI DI SAN GIUSEPPE

ST JOSEPH CREAM PUFFS

◆

- 150 G / 6 FL OZ / ¾ CUP WATER
- 100 G / 4 OZ / ⅔ CUP WHITE FLOUR
- 3 EGGS
- 100 G / 4 OZ / ¾ CUP ICING (CONFECTIONERS') SUGAR
- SACHET / ¼ TSP VANILLA POWDER / ½ TSP VANILLA EXTRACT
- 1 TBSP COGNAC
- 2 TBSP LARD OR 50 G / 2 OZ / 4 TBSP BUTTER
- GRATED ZEST OF 1 LEMON
- PINCH SALT
- OIL

THE FILLING:

- 500 G / 1 LB / 2¾ CUPS RICOTTA CHEESE
- 250 G / ½ LB / 1¼ CUPS GRANULATED SUGAR
- 100 G / 4 OZ / ½ CUP PLAIN (SEMI-SWEET) CHOCOLATE, DICED
- 50 G / 2 OZ / ¼ CUP CANDIED FRUIT
- 25 G / 1 OZ / 2 TBSP CANDIED ORANGE PEEL
- 25 G / 1 OZ / 2 TBSP PISTACHIOS, CHOPPED

◆

PREPARATION TIME: 3 HOURS

BRING THE WATER to the boil with the fat and salt, then throw in the flour, stirring well until thoroughly cooked (about 10 minutes). Remove the dough and spread it out over a work surface to cool rapidly. When cold, work in one egg yolk, add one stiffly-whisked egg white and, with a wooden spoon, continue mixing until incorporated. Repeat the procedure with the other two eggs.

The end result should be smooth and creamy. Pour plenty of oil into a deep frying pan and, when boiling, spoon in the dough to obtain soft, even-sized fritters. Once fried, allow to cool and slit each one open with a knife.

Meanwhile, work the ricotta into the icing sugar in a bowl and, if the mixture is too stiff, add a few drops of milk.

When the mixture is nice and creamy, add the chocolate and candied fruit.

Fill the cold "sfinci" and garnish with candied orange peel and the chopped pistachios.

TESTA DI TURCO

TORTA DI RISO
SWEET RICE PUDDING

◆

- 200 G / 8 OZ / 1 CUP RICE
- ½ L / 1 PT / 2 CUPS MILK
- 100 G / 4 OZ / ½ CUP GRANULATED SUGAR
- 2 EGGS, SEPARATED
- GRATED ZEST OF 1 LEMON
- 50 G / 2 OZ / ⅓ CUP RAISINS
- 1 SACHET / ¼ TSP VANILLA POWDER / ½ TSP VANILLA EXTRACT (OPTIONAL)
- DRY BREADCRUMBS
- OIL

◆

PREPARATION TIME: 3 HOURS
(ONLY 40 MINUTES IF YOU COOK
THE RICE A DAY AHEAD,
ADDING THE EGG YOLKS
THE FOLLOWING MORNING)

BOIL THE RICE for 5-6 minutes in salted water. Drain and continue cooking in another saucepan with the milk and a glass of water brought to the boil.

Add the sugar, the grated lemon zest and (if wished) the vanilla. When the rice is cooked, add the raisins tossed in flour, draw off the heat and allow to cool.

One at a time, incorporate the egg yolks into the rice, stirring well. Whisk the egg whites until stiff and fold into the mixture. Pour into an oiled-and-crumbed baking tin or dish and bake in a moderate oven for 30 minutes.

———

VARIATION: you can use the same mixture as a filling for a short pastry crust.

ZEPPOLE DI SEMOLINO

FRIED SEMOLINA

- ½ L / 1 PT / 2 CUPS MILK
- 300 G / ¾ LB / 2 CUPS SEMOLINA
- 150 G / 6 OZ / ¾ CUP GRANULATED SUGAR
- 30 G / 1 OZ / 2 TBSP ICING (CONFECTIONERS') SUGAR
- 30 G / 1 OZ / 2 TBSP SULTANAS OR RAISINS
- 1 LEMON
- PINCH CINNAMON
- HONEY
- ORANGE WATER
- FLOUR FOR COATING
- OIL FOR FRYING

PREPARATION TIME: 1 HOUR

IN A SAUCEPAN, bring the milk to boil with the granulated sugar and the grated lemon zest. Add the semolina and keep stirring (so that lumps do not form) until the mixture thickens.

Pour the dough onto a damp surface and, with a spatula, spread it out to a sheet half-an-inch thick. When it has cooled down completely, cut it into strips, coat with flour and fry in hot oil.

Dry on a kitchen paper towel, dust with icing sugar and cinnamon and trickle over the honey dissolved in a little water (orange water gives a nice fragrance).

This dessert is typical of Western Sicily and is also called "scocche di San Giuseppe" or St Joseph knots.

Finito di stampare
nel mese di Luglio 1996
presso il
CENTRO STAMPA EDITORIALE BONECHI
Sesto Fiorentino, Firenze

Contents

Disney on top

The Walt Disney Company is one of the best known, best loved and, just as importantly, most successful companies on the planet. In 2011, the latest instalment in the hit film series *Pirates of the Caribbean: On Stranger Tides*, starring Johnny Depp as pirate Jack Sparrow, passed $1 billion (£643m) in ticket sales worldwide and became the eighth highest grossing film ever released. (The *Pirates* franchise is based on a popular ride, opened nearly 50 years earlier in 1967, at Disneyland Park in Anaheim, California.)

And it wasn't just at the box office that Disney had a bumper year. Walt Disney Parks and Resorts worldwide brought in nearly $12 billion (£7.7bn), with revenue from TV networks, including sports network ESPN, Disney Channel and ABC Family contributing a further $19 billion (£12.2bn) to Disney's coffers.

With total 2011 revenues of $40.9bn (£26.3bn), and net profits of $4.8bn (£3.1bn) Disney is undoubtedly the largest media entertainment company in the world. In 2012 it did it again, breaking all box office record with Marvel's *Avengers Assemble*, which took $1.33bn (£855m) at box offices around the world, and became the third highest grossing film of all time behind *Avatar* and *Titanic*.

It's safe to say that everyone in the world has seen a Disney movie, watched a Disney-owned TV channel, visited a Disney theme park, or bought a Disney toy or game. The company's hold over

Johnny Depp and Penelope Cruz, stars of Pirates of the Caribbean: On Stranger Tides.

the world of entertainment is impressively large, and still growing.

Despite its modern, forward-thinking outlook, the Walt Disney Company owes its success to the hard work and vision of two men, Roy Disney and particularly his younger brother Walt, who were born over 100 years ago into a very different world. Both men had a dream – to entertain children and their parents, and to capture and maintain the magic and wonder of childhood. And it all started with a mouse...

> " All our dreams can come true, if we have the courage to pursue them. "
>
> **Walt Disney**

▼ *Huge crowds walk down the main street of Eurodisney in Paris.*

▼ *This pie chart shows revenues for 2011 across the entire Walt Disney Company.*

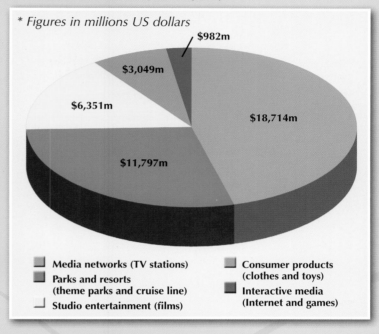

* *Figures in millions US dollars*

$982m
$3,049m
$6,351m
$18,714m
$11,797m

- ☐ **Media networks (TV stations)**
- ☐ **Parks and resorts** (theme parks and cruise line)
- ☐ **Studio entertainment (films)**
- ☐ **Consumer products** (clothes and toys)
- ☐ **Interactive media** (Internet and games)

The birth of Mickey Mouse

Today the Walt Disney Company spans the globe, but the origins of its founder and namesake are far more humble.

Walter Elias 'Walt' Disney was born on 5th December 1901, the youngest of five children. Young Walt spent his early years travelling the US, as his parents tried their luck at everything from gold prospecting to jam-making during the tough times of the American Depression. In his early teens, Walt became the cartoonist for his school newspaper in Chicago.

After leaving school he moved to Kansas City and found various jobs creating ads for newspapers and cinemas. At one of these, the Kansas City Film Ad Company, Walt produced early versions of TV commercials based on cut out animations. It sparked his own interest in animation and he started a company with colleague Fred Harman, producing cartoons called Laugh-O-Grams for a local cinema.

Unfortunately, Walt tried to grow his new company too quickly, hired too many animators, and went bust when new work failed to materialise. When the company closed, Walt and his older brother Roy put their savings together and moved to Hollywood – the film capital of the world! – to start a cartoon studio there.

▲ *Brothers Walt (left) and Roy Disney (right) discuss a bank loan for their business with the Bank of America's Vice President Bernard Giannini (centre).*

The pair's first successful animated character was called Oswald the Lucky Rabbit, created in 1927. However they failed to trademark Oswald, and eventually lost the rights to produce Oswald cartoons to Universal Studios who had funded and produced the series.

Business Matters

Copyright law — 'Copyright' — basically the right to copy or reproduce something — gives the creators of certain types of media the right to control how their creations are used and distributed. Music, books, video and computer software all be covered by copyright law. However, when the creation of a new cartoon character or song, for example, is paid for by a corporation rather than by an individual, it is the corporation that holds the copyright, as happened with Disney and the Oswald character.

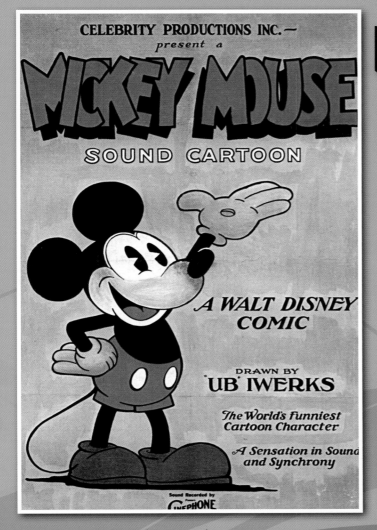

CELEBRITY PRODUCTIONS INC. —
present a

MICKEY MOUSE
SOUND CARTOON

A WALT DISNEY COMIC

DRAWN BY
UB IWERKS

The World's Funniest Cartoon Character

A Sensation in Sound and Synchrony

Sound Recorded by
CINEPHONE

▲ *An early advert for a Mickey Mouse cartoon.*

Brains Behind The Brand

Walt Disney – co-founder, Walt Disney Productions

Walt was the dreamer, the risk taker, and the driving creative force behind Disney's animation studio, motion pictures, and the creation of the first Disneyland theme park in Anaheim, California (see page 12).

Like all the best company heads, Walt was extremely focussed on his audience, and the Disney brand. He knew that Disney should deliver wonder, excitement and family fun, and everything the company made or produced stuck to those principles. In fact Walt's vision was so strong, that the company still stays extremely close to his original ideals many years after his death.

Walt was determined to create a new character to replace Oswald, and came up with a mouse – based on one that lived in his Laugh-O-Gram studio in Kansas City that he had adopted as a pet! Walt called him Mickey Mouse.

After two silent animated films starring Mickey, Disney created a Mickey cartoon with sound called *Steamboat Willie*. Cartoonist Ubbe Iwerks, who Walt knew from his animation days in Kansas City, drew Mickey, and Walt himself provided Mickey's voice. The result was a huge success, and Mickey quickly became the world's most popular cartoon character. By 1932 The Mickey Mouse Club had one million members, and just two years later Mickey merchandise was making $600,000 (£386,000) per year.

Snow White and the seven Oscars

Like all great businessmen and innovators, Walt Disney wasn't content with just one success, he was always striving for bigger and better things.

Mickey Mouse was Disney's first major success, winning a special Academy Award in 1932 and launching a long list of new characters including Goofy, Pluto, and Donald Duck, who quickly rivalled Mickey for popularity and became successful in their own right.

However, when Walt announced his plan to produce a full-length animated version of the Snow White fairytale, the film industry thought he was mad, and even his brother Roy and Walt's wife Lillian tried to talk him out of it. Everyone thought the animation costs on a full-length film would be restrictively high, but Walt persevered with his plans. *Snow White and the*

Seven Dwarfs eventually went into production in 1934, and carried on until mid-1937 when Disney ran out of money. Undeterred by this setback, Walt took a rough cut of the film to the Bank of America to apply for a loan to finish the film!

The application was accepted, *Snow White* was finished and finally released in February 1938, becoming the most successful film of the year and earning over $8m (the equivalent of £122m today). The picture won an honorary Academy Award for screen innovation, and Walt was presented with an Oscar – and seven miniatures – to mark the achievement.

▼ *A scene from Disney's* Snow White and the Seven Dwarfs, *the world's first animated film.*

The profits from *Snow White* helped Disney build a huge new Walt Disney Studios complex in Burbank, California, which is still home to the company today. It also funded further full-length animations — *Pinocchio* and *Fantasia* were released in 1940, and *Dumbo* in 1941.

By December 1941, the United States had entered World War II. During the war production slowed dramatically as Disney and many of his animators were called up to help the war effort. By 1942, 90% of the company's 550 employees were working on war-related films. These films were great for morale, but didn't generate income for Disney, and by the end of the war, the studio's bank account was looking worryingly empty!

▼ *Walt's eight Oscars — one large and seven small — that he was awarded for* Snow White.

Brains Behind The Brand

Roy Disney – co-founder, Walt Disney Productions

If Walt was the creative force behind Disney, Roy was the businessman. Roy became Disney CEO in 1929, and shared the Chairman of the Board role with Walt until 1960.

Bringing Walt's visions to life cost a lot of money, and it was Roy's job to keep accurate accounts, make sure bills were paid, and ensure that the young company had enough money to pay its staff and invest in new projects. This role would probably have been given the title of Chief Financial Officer (CFO) in most companies.

When Walt died in 1966, Roy (who was 74 himself) came out of retirement to oversee completion of Walt Disney World, and ran the company until his own death in 1971.

> " All the adversity I've had in my life, all my troubles and obstacles, have strengthened me. You may not realise it when it happens, but a kick in the teeth may be the best thing in the world for you. "
> **Walt Disney**

Many companies occasionally suffer from cashflow problems. Often they have to change or adapt their plans to take these into account. In Disney's case, their problems led to further success.

After WWII, Disney and his animators returned to the studio full time. However, the war years had meant minimal film production, and therefore minimal income. It was clear that they didn't have the funds to start producing more full-length animated films straight away, so they concentrated on 'package films' (collections of already existing short films, edited together so that they could be sold into cinemas), as well as live-action films and documentaries, such as *Seal Island* (1948), which were cheaper to produce than animation.

By the end of the decade, Disney had recovered sufficiently to start work on several new animated films, *Alice In Wonderland* (1951), *Peter Pan* (1953), and *Cinderella* (1950), which became the company's most successful release since *Snow White*. Disney Studios also produced several successful live-action films throughout the 1950s, including *Treasure Island* (1950), *The Shaggy Dog* (1959) and *Swiss Family Robinson* (1960), and peaking with *Mary Poppins* in 1964, which won five Oscars, including Best Actress for Julie Andrews.

▼ *Walt Disney (left) discusses the soundtrack to* Fantasia *with the film's composer Deems Taylor (middle) and conductor Leopold Stokowski (right).*

▲ *A still from Disney's* Song of the South, *which mixed live action with animation.*

However, it was the rise of television that really provided Disney's biggest new opportunities for growth. In 1950, Walt Disney Productions and the Coca-Cola Company teamed up to produce a one-hour special for NBC television, called *An Hour In Wonderland*. New opportunities to find Disney fans in every living room in the US opened up to Walt, and by 1954 Disney launched its *Disneyland* series on ABC, a mixture of live action and animation that gave Disney the chance to raid its archive as well as introduce new characters and ideas.

By 1955, the studio's first daily show, *Mickey Mouse Club*, launched on ABC. Produced under Walt's direct supervision, it was a groundbreaking mix of comedy, music and drama aimed completely at children. Walt even went back into the studio himself to record Mickey Mouse's voice. The show was a huge success, running around the world for many years, and even appearing on the Disney Channel into the 1990s, where it launched the careers of the singers Britney Spears, Christina Aguilera and Justin Timberlake and the actor Ryan Gosling.

Business Matters

Diversification — companies often decide to offer new products or services — as when Disney moved into television production — because it reduces the risk of its other business interests becoming too limited or uninteresting. By adding television production to its animation studio, Disney gave consumers more reasons to engage with the Disney brand. When companies offer a completely different product or service, like supermarkets offering car or house insurance, this is called 'brandstretching'.

▼ *This pie chart shows income from subscription channels by value in US dollars.*

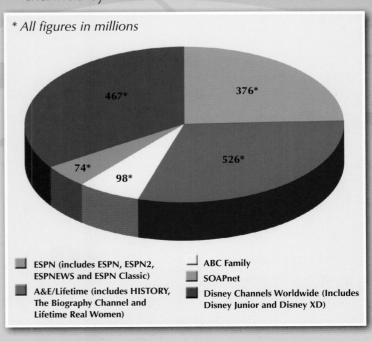

* All figures in millions

467*   376*   526*   98*   74*

■ ESPN (includes ESPN, ESPN2, ESPNEWS and ESPN Classic)

■ A&E/Lifetime (includes HISTORY, The Biography Channel and Lifetime Real Women)

◻ ABC Family

■ SOAPnet

■ Disney Channels Worldwide (Includes Disney Junior and Disney XD)

The birth of the theme parks

Since the late 1940s, Walt had been dreaming up ideas for an amusement park that adults could enjoy as much as their children. The project became known as Disneyland.

A great believer in family entertainment, Walt became fascinated with the idea of a theme park where his employees could take their children and enjoy time together. He was inspired by the opening of the Children's Fairyland in Oakland, California and initially planned to build his own park on vacant land across the road from the Disney offices in Burbank.

As usual, Walt's plans grew more and more ambitious and cost estimates started to rise. To safeguard the finances of Walt Disney Productions, Walt and Roy created a new company, WED Enterprises, that would carry out planning and production for the park. A carefully selected group of Disney studio employees also joined the project as engineers and planners, and were nicknamed 'the Imagineers'.

Walt and Roy succeeded in winning television network ABC's financial backing for the project and in 1955 – after five years of building – the Disneyland Park in Anaheim, California opened to the public. On the opening day, 18 July 1955, Walt gave a speech:

'Disneyland is dedicated to the ideals, the dreams and the hard facts that have created America... with the hope that it will be a source of joy and inspiration to all the world.'

▼ *Sleeping Beauty's Castle under construction at Disneyland in 1955.*

Brains Behind The Brand

Thomas Staggs – Chairman, Walt Disney Parks and Resorts

Staggs oversees Disney's worldwide holiday and travel business, which includes a cruise line, holiday resorts, and 11 theme parks in five locations across the US, Europe and Asia. He took over the role in January 2010, and was previously Disney's Chief Financial Officer (CFO), in charge of areas including worldwide finances and company acquisitions (see page 25).

Staggs joined Disney in 1990 as Manager of Strategic Planning, becoming CFO in 1998. He played a major part in Disney's acquisitions of TV network Capital Cities/ABC, and film studios Pixar and Marvel.

Demand grew for Disney theme parks around the world, and in April 1992 Disneyland Paris opened to the public. The cost of building parks is extremely high, and Disney usually shares the costs – and therefore the ownership – with a local partner. Disney owns 39.78% of Disneyland Paris shares, and 43% of the shares in Shanghai Disney Resort, a $4.4bn development in China that is due to launch in December 2015.

The opportunity for Disney fans around the world to experience Walt's dream firsthand is a huge part of what makes the brand so successful and loved.

> " Disneyland is a work of love. We didn't go into Disneyland just with the idea of making money. "
>
> **Walt Disney**

Disneyland is divided into several different worlds, with a stylised and nostalgic vision of America that adults love, and funfair rides that are exciting enough to challenge everyone's courage. Add to that the appearance, several times a day, of life-size Disney characters, from Mickey Mouse to Tigger, and it's not surprising that Disneyland now attracts around 16m visitors per year.

By 1965 Disney was ready to expand, and plans to launch 'Disney World' in Orlando, Florida, were announced. Walt Disney World today contains four theme parks, two water parks, 23 on-site hotels and five golf courses, and is the world's most visited entertainment resort with close to 17m visitors per year to its Magic Kingdom.

Mickey and Minnie Mouse in traditional dress at Tokyo's Disneyland.

Life and death at Disney

Some companies are built around the vision and personality of one man – like Steve Jobs at Apple, or Walt at Disney. Yet they also need to survive after the death of their founder and figurehead.

On 2 November 1966, Walt underwent X-rays before routine surgery on an old neck injury. Doctors discovered a tumour on his left lung, and further tests showed it to be malignant. Walt underwent emergency surgery and chemotherapy, and returned home to recuperate. Unfortunately, on 30 November he collapsed at his home and on 15 December, just ten days after his 65th birthday, he died.

Before his illness, Walt had been as busy as ever. He was supervising construction of Disney World Resort in Florida, plans for a new ski resort in Sequoia National Forest, and renovations of Disneyland in Anaheim, as well as six motion pictures, and countless television productions.

Throughout his life, Walt held no formal title at Disney, but he was unquestionably the boss. Under his leadership, Disney had won 29 Oscars and four Emmys, and Walt himself had been awarded the Presidential Freedom Medal. Nevertheless, brother Roy was determined to carry on the Disney legacy as smoothly as possible. In 1967 he released the final two films with which Walt had been actively involved, the musical *The Happiest Millionaire* and *The Jungle Book*.

Mowgli with friends Baloo the bear and Bagheera the panther in a scene from The Jungle Book.

The entire staff of Walt Disney World pose for a photograph before the grand opening of the theme park in 1971.

> We will continue to operate Walt's company in the way that he had established and guided it. All of the plans for the future that Walt had begun will continue to move ahead.
>
> **Roy Disney**

Roy also kept Walt's amusement park dream alive and saw through plans to finish the Florida theme park. Walt Disney World, named in Walt's honour, was opened in October 1971. Two months later Roy died from a stroke and the running of the company passed to long-time Disney executives Donn Tatum and Card Walker, both trained by Roy and Walt.

Management continuity is often important for large businesses, and when Donn Tatum became Disney CEO after Roy's death, he had already worked at Disney for 15 years. So despite being the first non-Disney family member to be company president, he was well trained in the core values of Disney. Tatum played an important role in the development of the Walt Disney World Resort and EPCOT Center in Florida, as well as Tokyo Disneyland. Card Walker had been with Disney even longer, joining the company's post room in 1938! Between Tatum and Walker, they were at the head of Disney until 1983.

For a company as well-established as Disney, it has had very few Presidents since its launch in 1923.

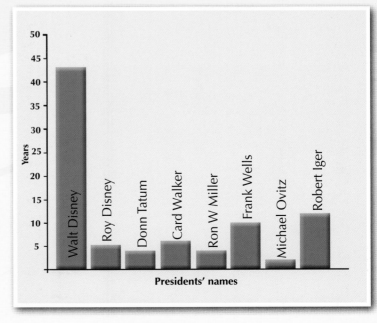

The theme parks are the public face of Disney. But it's the Walt Disney Studios in Burbank that are the real heart of the Disney empire, housing management offices, film stages and animation studios.

When Walt and Roy Disney moved to Los Angeles in the summer of 1923, they set up their first office in the garage of their Uncle Robert in an area called Los Feliz. By 1925, with distribution secured on a new animated series called *Alice Comedies*, Walt invested in larger office space at 2719 Hyperion Avenue. By 1940, they were ready to move again, and Walt reinvested the profits from *Snow White* to build the Walt Disney Studios in Burbank.

There are around 15,000 employees (Disney prefers to call them 'cast members') working at the Walt Disney Studios. This includes animators, set builders, office staff, film producers, TV executives and many more. The site contains many of the original animation buildings from the 1940s, as well as sound stages (warehouse-sized, soundproof buildings where films are made), staff offices and restaurants.

▼ *An aerial view of the Walt Disney Studios in Burbank, California.*

Current president and CEO of Disney, Robert Iger, has an office in the Michael D Eisner Building, which is named after the former head of Disney who ran the company for 21 years. Alongside Iger, there are offices for Rich Ross, Chairman of the Walt Disney Studios, Thomas Staggs, Chairman of Walt Disney Parks, and Andy Bird, Chairman of Walt Disney International.

Outside the Eisner Building is the Disney Legends Plaza, containing statues of Walt with Mickey Mouse, and Roy with Minnie. Bronze plaques commemorate valued Disney animators and 'Imagineers', with their hand prints and signatures set into the bronze.

Across from the Plaza is the Frank G Wells Building, named after the former Disney President. The Wells Building houses Disney's TV animation department, the company archives (a museum of Disney memorabilia) and the Human Resources (HR) department.

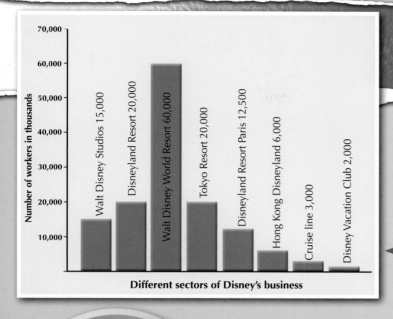

Cast members usually eat lunch in one of the two restaurants on site. The Studio Commissary serves chilli every day in memory of Walt, who often came in for a bowl, even on the hottest of California days. There is also a Starbucks coffee shop and a Disney Store for cast members only!

◄ *This graph shows the number of workers or 'cast members' who were employed in the various sectors of Disney's business in 2011.*

Business Matters

Human Resources — The Human Resources (HR) department of a company is responsible for putting in place and maintaining the business practices that allow effective people management. Some key responsibilities of an HR department are: 1) training; 2) staff appraisal: a formal process, performed by managers on their staff, which aims to communicate how they are performing and to discuss what they need in order to improve and develop; 3) staff development: the processes in the company designed to identify the people with potential, keep them in the organization, and move them into the right positions.

◄ *Animator Marc Segan, with early Disney artwork from 'Steamboat Willie'.*

Disney grows up

By the 1980s it was clear that Disney needed to modernise and bring in new blood to face the business challenges ahead. A failed takeover attempt was just the motivation they needed to make changes fast!

Throughout the 1970s and early 1980s, Disney carried on producing a mix of animated and live action films, including the futuristic *Tron* in 1982. Its success led to then Disney CEO Ron Miller, Walt's son-in-law, creating a new brand, Touchstone Pictures, which could release more adult-oriented films, like *Splash* (1984) with Tom Hanks.

In 1983, Disney launched the subscription-only Disney Channel, featuring its archive of classic films and TV shows. Works also continued with Walt's dream for a space-age city, which became the EPCOT Center in Florida.

Despite the success of the Disney Channel and its theme parks, Disney was falling behind its Hollywood competitors, and the management team, led by 50-year old Miller, was often criticised for lacking vision and ambition. In 1984, a US

▲ *Jeffrey Katzenberg (left) and Michael Eisner at the opening of Disney's Beauty and the Beast.*

businessman called Saul Steinberg launched a 'hostile takeover' bid with the aim of buying Disney and selling off its various parts – theme parks, movie archive and so on– to the highest bidders.

Disney managed to fight off the bid thanks to friendly investors, but the management, including Roy's son, Roy E Disney, realised that they needed to strengthen the management team and plan for the future, and so hired Michael Eisner and Jeffrey Katzenberg from Paramount Pictures, and Frank Wells from Warner Brothers.

Business Matters

Company directors — Company directors, often called a board of directors, oversee the activities of a company. A board's role is determined by the powers and responsibilities given to it by a company's own rules and regulations. These rules usually cover the number of members of the board, how they are chosen, and how often they meet. The board usually chooses one of its members to be the Chairman (or 'President' in the US). Typical duties of a board include: setting the rules that run the organization; selecting, appointing, supporting and reviewing the performance of the chief executive; approving annual budgets; reporting to shareholders on the company's performance.

Brains Behind The Brand

Rich Ross – Chairman, the Walt Disney Studios

Ross oversees all new production from the Pixar, Marvel and Disney film studios, as well as marketing and distribution for the independent DreamWorks Studios. In recent years, this has included massive global hits from Disney's *Alice in Wonderland and Pirates of the Caribbean: On Stranger Tides* to Marvel's *Avengers Assemble*.

Before joining Disney Studios in 2009, Ross was President of Disney Channels Worldwide, and was responsible for original programmes such as *Hannah Montana, High School Musical, Phineas and Ferb* and *Wizards of Waverley Place*, which contributed to a massive growth in Disney's TV business.

The new management team brought the dynamism and energy to Disney that had been lacking for a few years. Under Michael Eisner's management from 1984-2005, Disney experienced strong growth and consolidation, starting with the successes of films *Who Framed Roger Rabbit* (1988), which won three Oscars, including for best visual effects and sound effects editing, and *The Little Mermaid* (1989).

At the start of the 1990s, Eisner announced plans for 'The Disney Decade', which included existing park expansions, new parks being built, new film franchises and new media investments.

Over the next few years, Disney bought Miramax Pictures in 1993, released the Oscar-winning *The Lion King* (1994), merged with Capital Cities/ABC on the TV side in 1996 (which brought in ABC and ESPN sports network), and launched new theme parks in Hong Kong and Paris. When Eisner finally stepped down in 2005, his role was taken by his long-time assistant, Robert Iger – once again ensuring continuity within the company.

◄ In 1994, 'Can you feel the love tonight' from The Lion King *won the Oscar for best song for Elton John (left) and Tim Rice (right).*

'The best 30 minutes of a child's day'

When the first Disney Store opened in 1987, Disney finally entered the world of retail. Fortunes have risen and fallen over the years, but now appear to be back on top.

The first Disney Store opened in Glendale, California in March 1987. The idea was so successful that the company quickly expanded to over 600 stores around the world. However, in some cases, Disney opened as many as five stores in the same town, and sales just couldn't keep up with store running costs. By 2002, Disney stores were losing around $100m (£64m) per year.

Large and successful companies will often support a division that is losing money, but Disney management decided instead to license the business, which means they sold the rights to use the Disney name to another company. The

Children's Place, who bought the licence, had to operate under strict rules laid down by Disney regarding the merchandise they sold in Disney Stores, and the prices they charged.

Unfortunately, the partnership was not a success. The Children's Place believed it could not run the business in the way it wanted to and Disney did not feel that the stores accurately reflected the Disney brand. So in 2008, Disney 'bought back' its own stores, closing some of the less successful ones in the chain.

When Disney bought Pixar Studios in 2006, they granted a place on their board of directors to

▼ *A trademark Disney Store, decorated for Christmas.*

▲ *Bob Chapek (fourth on the right) with cast members at a party to celebrate a Hollywood screening of* High School Musical.

Steve Jobs, Pixar's owner and the man who had revitalised the fortunes of computer company Apple and launched the extremely successful Apple stores.

With Jobs' help, the President of Disney Stores, Jim Fielding, announced a five-year plan to turn the Disney shopping experience into 'the best 30 minutes of a child's day'. It's estimated that Disney will spend $1m (£640,000) per store to modernise its whole chain. Stores will include 'Magic Mirrors' that speak to children holding princesses' tiaras, and interactive displays will show Disney films and TV shows on touch-screens.

Brains Behind The Brand

Bob Chapek – President, Disney Consumer Products (DCP)

Disney has its name and images on more products than any other company in the world – from clothes, toys and stationery to food, drink and home furnishings. Chapek oversees this large and complicated business, which includes Walt Disney Studios, Pixar and now Marvel Comics. His job is to maximise revenues while ensuring that products are good quality and meet customers' needs.

Chapek became President of Consumer Products in 2011 after two years as President of Distribution for Walt Disney Studios, where he was involved in overseeing new movies through cinema releases, onto DVD, then subscription channels and new media. In this role he set several sales records in the straight-to-video business that included *High School Musical* and its sequels.

Business Matters

Long-term success — successful companies are 'market-driven', in other words they focus on satisfying the exact section of the market in which they are operating. All of Disney's different companies — from television to theme parks — have to make sure that they provide something that visitors or viewers ('the market') want. Successful companies also need to be 'sustainable', meaning that people not only want to buy or use their products now, but that they will continue to want to use them in the future.

Disney gets interactive

Interactive entertainment – another name for computer and social media games – is an important part of Disney's business strategy, helping the company connect with fans through their game consoles and now mobile phones.

Disney followed the explosion in the video games industry in the 1980s by launching its own division to focus on the development of computer and video games, Walt Disney Computer Software, in 1988.

At first, Disney worked mainly as a games developer, coding and designing new games featuring Disney cartoon and film characters, and relying on business agreements with games publishers such as Sony, Nintendo and others to manufacture and distribute the games.

In 2003, Disney's games division brought production and distribution in-house, and rebranded as Buena Vista Games. One part of the company, Buena Vista Interactive, focussed on multi-platform games for teens and adults, while Disney Interactive specialised in children's entertainment and learning software. Buena Vista Games' biggest success was a series of action role-playing games called *Kingdom Hearts*, which has sold 17 million copies worldwide and launched spin-off magazines, figurines and even a music soundtrack.

◄ *The Disney Dreamsketcher, just one of many Disney interactive toys and games.*

As cinema audiences began to reduce and CD sales kept falling, interactive games companies have become more profitable than the traditional entertainment areas of film and music. Games developers such as Take-Two Interactive (who produce the *Bioshock* and *Grand Theft Auto* series) are generating revenues of over $1bn (£640m) per year, and social games developer Zynga, which makes games like *FarmVille* and *CityVille*, which can be played on mobile phones or through users' Facebook pages, makes over $600m (£383m) per year.

Disney's games division was keen to take a slice of this growing market, and rebranded again in 2007, becoming Disney Interactive Media Group (DIMG - pronounced 'dim-gee'). In 2010, it purchased Playdom, a successful social game developer with 47 million monthly users, for over $500m (£320m).

▼ Despite growing revenues, DIMG has made a loss every year since its launch.

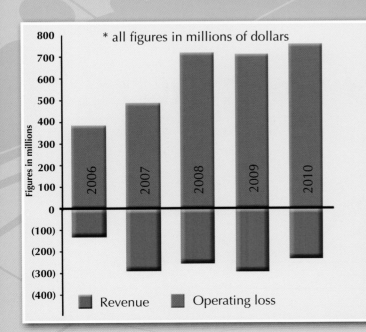

Despite the investment in Playdom, DIMG is currently one of Disney's few non-profitable divisions. Since January 2011 it has made over 200 employees redundant, and in the first three months of 2012, announced a $28m (£17.8m) loss. DIMG is now shifting production away from expensive console games towards online and mobile gaming, but only time will tell if it will bring success to what is still a troubled Disney division.

Brains Behind The Brand

John Pleasants – Co-President, Disney Interactive Media Group

Pleasants runs two Disney divisions – DIMG, the interactive entertainment section that focuses on console and mobile games, and Playdom, which produced Disney's social media games. He oversees the creation and development of all new games, and is in regular contact with Disney's global network of game developers to make sure that he gets the best, must-buy products first.

Pleasants was previously the CEO of Playdom, which was bought by Disney in 2010. Before joining Playdom, he was President of Publishing and Chief Operating Officer (COO) of games company Electronic Arts, where he was in charge of global sales. Pleasants has also worked at major websites Ticketmaster and Match.com.

Steadying the ship

Under current CEO and Chairman Bob Iger, Disney has continued to grow and prosper, keeping its connections with the company's rich traditions, but always looking to the future.

Since Iger took over from Michael Eisner, Disney has gone through a period of modernising and adapting to the changes in consumer tastes. This has meant embracing the possibilities of computer animation and 3D film-making, and moving away from Disney's hand-drawn animation. 'I really believe the company should look at technology as a friend,' explains Iger. 'It had been part of the company originally. Walt Disney was a big believer in technology.'

Iger's first step was to invest in the company's long-term film-making success, buying Pixar for $7.4bn (£4.7bn) in 2006, and Marvel Entertainment for $4.2bn (£2.7bn) in 2009. Both studios focussed on the strong storytelling and family-friendly releases that have always been Disney's trademark. At the same time, the Miramax and Touchstone brands were sold or downsized, and the company's loss-making divisions (like DIMG) were also cut back.

More recently, Iger has made positive steps to tap into the fast-growing Far East market, working hard to secure the support of the Chinese government to start work on the Shanghai Disney Resort, which is scheduled to open in 2015. In 2012, Disney bought UTV Software

◄ *An artist's impression of a completed Shanghai Disney Resort, scheduled to open in 2015.*

▲ Iron Man *was a big cinema hit for Disney in 2008.*

Communications, an Indian multimedia company, producing films, TV, website, games and animation, in order to keep expanding Disney's business into Asia.

With over 160 million members of Disney Facebook groups, Iger has taken the opportunity to engage with these fans, find out what they are thinking, and use their feedback for valuable market research. Iger is as big a Disney fan as any of them, but he realises that the company is competing in the 21st century, and that simply 'doing what Walt did' is not going to take the company to further success.

Disney today is at the height of its powers. The challenge now for Iger, and the whole company, is to keep growing and keep innovating, while staying faithful to the ideals that makes Disney such a magical, well-loved brand.

Brains Behind The Brand

Robert Iger – Chairman and CEO, the Walt Disney Company

As Chairman of Disney, Iger is responsible for one of the world's best-loved brands. His job is to keep the company growing and thriving, but every decision he makes is based on three important principles: generating the best content possible; innovating and using the latest technology available; expanding into new markets around the world.

With the purchase of Pixar in 2006 and Marvel Comics in 2009, Iger has remained loyal to Walt Disney's goal of focussing on great storytelling. He has also helped make the company an industry leader in creating content across multiple platforms – from cinema and DVD to mobile phones and tablets.

Iger began his career in 1974 with US television channel ABC, and worked his way to the top, becoming chairman of ABC in 1996. In 1999 he was promoted to President, Walt Disney International, then Chairman and CEO in 2005.

Business Matters

Mergers and acquisitions — This phrase refers to the aspect of company strategy and finance that deals with the buying, selling and combining of different companies. This strategy can help a company grow rapidly within its market without having to create another separate company. An acquisition is the purchase of one company by another company, as when Disney bought Pixar in 2006 and Playdom in 2010. A merger is when two companies combine to form a third, new company.

Business success is based on constantly moving forward – assessing what works and doesn't work, and acting accordingly. Here's how we predict Disney will change in the next few years.

It's safe to assume that Disney will focus its efforts on several key areas, as follows:

Film franchises

Disney's huge success with the first *Avengers* movie is sure to lead to further Marvel films. *Iron Man 3* was released in early 2013, with *Thor 2* coming out later in the year. They will be followed by the second *Captain America* film, and an inevitable *Avengers* sequel. There are also new Marvel adaptations promised,

including *Guardians of the Galaxy* and *Ant-Man*.

International expansion

Disney has already taken the significant step of starting work on a new theme park in Shanghai, which it plans to open by 2015. There are also plans to open a smaller park in Haifa, Israel. Hong Kong Disneyland has announced that three new 'lands' will be added to the park – Grizzly Gulch, Mystic Point and Toy Story Land.

◀ *In 2011 Disney released The Muppets, starring Jason Segel and Amy Adams. The film made over $100 million worldwide.*

"
'If you can dream it, you can do it.'
Walt Disney
"

Brains Behind The Brand

Andy Bird – Chairman, Walt Disney International

Bird has three main areas of responsibility: targeting existing businesses for Disney to buy; increasing Disney's market share and profitability in the main markets of Western Europe and Japan; and leading Disney's development into new, 'emerging' markets like India, China and Russia.

Bird joined Disney in 2004, and one of his first deals was the purchase of Indian TV station Hungama TV in order to grow Disney's visibility in the region. He has also worked for global TV and entertainment company Time Warner, where he was in charge of their TV channels.

Updating US parks

In September 2011, Disney secured exclusive global theme parks rights to director James Cameron's *Avatar*. Plans were immediately announced to partner with 20th Century Fox, and Cameron's production company, Lightstorm Entertainment, to build theme park attractions based on the blockbusting film. The first ride is planned for Disney's Animal Kingdom at Walt Disney World, Florida. The park is also due for further new rides, including a *Little Mermaid* ride, and a *Seven Dwarfs' Mine Train* ride.

More cruise line destinations

Disney will also focus on its holiday and resort business, and are planning to add a new cruise – from Los Angeles to Hawaii – to their itinerary. They are also adding new home ports in New York City and Galveston, making it easier for passengers to join Atlantic and Caribbean cruises.

Advances in technology

Disney will undoubtedly use advances in technology to attract and engage new fans. New apps will allow Disney Channel subscribers to watch the Disney Channel, Disney XD and Disney Junior on their handheld devices. DIMG's focus will also be on building an online community of loyal Disney fans that will grow up with the brand, just as children have been doing since the 1930s.

Although no company's continued success is ever guaranteed, Disney's future looks to be in safe hands. Here's to the next 100 years!

◄ *Disney Stores worldwide are being modernised and made more interactive.*

To create a new product, it is helpful to produce a product development brief like the one below. This is a sample brief for a new theme park ride called Iron Man. The SWOT analysis on the page opposite will help you to think about the strengths, weaknesses, opportunities and threats for your product. This can help you to see how feasible and practical your idea is before you think of investing time and money in it.

Product Development Brief

Name of product: Iron Man 'Total Experience' Ride

Type of product: Theme park ride for Disney resorts worldwide

The product explained (use 25 words or less): This new ride brings the Iron Man movies to life – experience flying and super strength in your own Iron Man bodysuit.

Target age of users: 15-45

What does the product do? This ride is actually a simulator, but instead of placing all participants into a rollercoaster carriage in front of a video screen, each person using Iron Man puts on their own suit, and has the video screen projected onto the inside of the goggles they are wearing. Additional movements are made by standing on a motion simulator and operating pressure points from inside the suit.

Are there any similar products already available? None

What makes your product different? It's the first motion simulator 'ride' that gives the passenger the experience of being fully immersed in a game.

Name of product you are assessing . . . Iron Man 'Total Experience' Ride
The table below will help you assess your Disney theme park ride. By addressing all four areas, you can make your product stronger and more likely to be a success.

Questions to consider	Strengths
Does your ride do something unique?	*It's the only ride of its kind in the world.*
Is there anything innovative about it? What are its USPs (unique selling points)?	*Simulator rides and using goggles are not new, but no one has provided a full immersion simulation for the price of a theme park ride.*

	Weaknesses
Why wouldn't people use this ride? Can everyone use it?	*The Iron Man 'Total Experience' will have age limits and height restrictions. It may also require a basic health check, and perhaps blood pressure to be taken, before park visitors can use it.*
Are there any dangers associated with the ride?	*Some users may experience motion sickness.*
Do you need additional trained members of staff to monitor customers when they use the ride in case they have problems with it?	*Iron Man suits are expensive to make, and so only limited numbers will be available at each park. Therefore queues could be very long to be able to use one.*

	Opportunities
Can the ride be improved in the future, eg better graphics, or motion simulation?	*As technology gets even more realistic, and cheaper to produce, the ride can become better, and cheaper over time.*
Can the ride be used at Disney parks worldwide?	*Theme parks worldwide can use the suit, as there are no language barriers.*
Can it develop new USPs?	*New technology advances could introduce new experiences to the suit, eg feeling hot, cold, wind on the skin, that would improve the experience.*

	Threats
Is the market that you are selling in to shrinking?	*No, the market will keep growing.*
Will the ride face competition from other theme parks?	*Other parks will develop rides based on other blockbuster films.*
Are any of your weaknesses so bad they might affect the ride in the long run?	*The technology will be untried at first, and may well experience breakdowns and leave suits out of action. Hopefully they can be fixed quickly, or customers will lose confidence in the ride.*

Do you have what it takes to work at Disney? Try this!

1. Are you a fan of cartoons and animation?
a) No, cartoons are for little kids! I left that behind at pre-school.
b) I like *Spongebob Square Pants*. Does that count?
c) Yes, love it! I think animation can be a fun and immediate way of telling a story to all generations.

2. Do you like theme parks and theme park rides?
a) Ooh, they're too scary for me! I like to keep my feet on the ground.
b) I've been to the odd one on school trips, and I try to visit new rides when they open.
c) Yes, I've even been to Walt Disney World in Florida. It's magical. I can't wait to go back!

3. When was the last time you went to the cinema?
a) I'm not a big cinemagoer. I prefer watching football, or playing video games at home.
b) I go 5-6 times a year – usually with a big group of friends. We enjoy the experience of being together as much as the films we watch.
c) I go all the time! I keep up with all the latest releases – especially action and fantasy films.

4) Have you ever come up with an idea that you thought would make a great film?
a) Mmm, I prefer hearing other people's ideas rather than coming up with my own.
b) I sometimes read books and think they would make great films. *Hunger Games*, for example!
c) I did actually have a great idea for a story with loads of new characters that I think people would love. Help me get it made into a film!

5. What's your favourite subject at school?
a) Food technology. Oh, and I like Games.
b) Probably history. I enjoy learning about old civilisations and how people lived in ancient times.
c) I enjoy English. Creative writing is a big favourite of mine. I love coming up with fantastic ideas about interesting people.

6. What do you want to do when you leave school?
a) I'm planning to work for the family business. That way I can take days off whenever I want and not get sacked.
b) I want to go to university, and then hopefully become a teacher.
c) I'd love to work for a big global corporation that affects millions of people's lives. I'm prepared to work very hard to get to the top!

Results
Mostly As: Sorry, but your chances of working at Disney are looking shaky! It doesn't sound like you have the interest in Disney's main business areas to succeed at this world-famous company.

Mostly Bs: You are thoughtful and hard-working, but you need to work on your motivation and individuality if you want to succeed in a very competitive business.

Mostly Cs: It sounds like you have what it takes to get a job at Disney. Keep working hard at school, and pushing to be the best, and who knows?

Glossary

adaptation film versions of a book, or comic book.

archive a collection of older programmes that can be reused or re-edited.

bumper exceptionally large or successful.

cashflow the amount of money a company has in the bank at a given time.

coffers the funds or financial reserves of a company.

commemorating recalling or showing respect to something or someone.

computer chip an electronic circuit that forms the basis of many electronic devices.

core values most deeply or passionately held beliefs.

downsized made a company smaller by reducing staff numbers.

dynamism positivity, hard-working attitude.

embracing willingly or enthusiastically accepting something.

franchise a well-known or important brand name, for example *The Avengers*, which can make money in different media, from films, games, merchandise and so on.

futuristic involving modern or advanced technology.

grossing a figure without costs (for example production costs) taken off. Film can gross £100m, but if they cost £120m to make, then they lose money!

honorary a special award to recognise achievement.

humble modest, unimportant, unimpressive.

inevitable certain to happen, unavoidable.

initially at first.

innovator someone who introduces new methods, ideas or products into an existing business.

instalment a part of something, for example one film in a series about the same character or characters.

itinerary a planned route or journey.

malignant describes a tumour that is spreading.

materialise to happen, become real

merchandise products used to promote a film, cartoon character, etc. Can include posters, action figures and so on.

minimal a small or insignificant amount.

modernise to adapt or change something for modern tastes or interests.

net profits profits after all costs have been taken into account.

nostalgic feeling happy memories about the past, or one's childhood

persevere to keep trying with little or no chance of success.

revenue income, money coming in to a company.

strive to make great efforts to achieve something.

subscription a membership or monthly payment.

trademark to legally register the ownership of something.

undeterred persevering with something despite setbacks.

went bust went bankrupt, lost all one's money.

Index